TELEGRAPH POLE
APPRECIATION
FOR
BEGINNERS

by Martin Evans

For Mathew
To the man who thought
he had everything.

Martin Evans

Printed in a lovely part of lovely Wales,
part of the lovely United Kingdom

First Published 2017

ISBN 978 1 9998491 0 8

Arenig Press
Dolfawr
Cwmrheidol
Aberystwyth
Ceredigion
SY23 3NB

www.arenig.co.uk

Printed by: Cambrian Printers, Aberystwyth, lovely Wales.

To everyone...
who ever did even the tiniest thing for me.
And to K who did everything else.

Thanks also to contributors. In no particular order:

John Cranston, James Bancroft, Russ Firth, John
Brunsden, Jake Rideout, Ben Wells, Gene Kingsley,
Willie Montgomery Stack, Graeme Donkin, Pete
Gerrard, Bradley Wells, Adrian Trainsett, Keith S****,
Dave Bennett (#666), Agent #0650 +mum, Pete
Greenrod, Kev Currie, James Bancroft (again), Quorn
online museum, Doreen Bracegirdle (Mrs)

BT Heritage & Archives.

and to all our photographic contributors over the
years - sorry if your photo missed out.

Thanks also to Keri (for patience), Debbie (Keri's
sister, for typos), our Hâf (for loving it), John
Cranston (grammar and general pulling to bits),
Bryan (for not rubbishing it)

Lost in France
Telegraph poles
photo © James Bancroft

Page One

Tradition has it that a book should have an introduction. A preface perhaps. A few paragraphs that might explain the point of said book. Some waffle of why I wrote it, what's in it and what wisdom you might accrue from the pages that follow. What's the difference between a Preface and an Introduction anyway? I could have had both. I chose neither. And what about a Foreword? These are usually written by some illuminati or person of renown but the closest I ever got to fame was when I overtook Olympic swimmer Duncan Goodhew on the M6 near Walsall.

Consider though the benefits of a book wholly without any kind of preamble. That's at least a whole page that hasn't needed to be produced. There's a carbon offset benefit here. Over the anticipated fourteen million copies of this book sold, that is a forest equivalent to 1¼ Wales worth of trees saved – if my calculator missing the #4 key serves me correct. Also no energy used in the printing of the missing page, no barrels of ink needed to be transported to the printers - at least a thousand road miles saved here or 10,000 miles if I choose not to have it printed in New Zealand. Not to mention the energy conserved by you carrying less weight home from the book shop, and having the light on for shorter time as you don't read the missing page. So as well as the myriad book and literary prizes for this effort, I am also anticipating a gargantuan award from Greenpeace for not having any kind of introduction whatsoever.

It's about telegraph poles.

Martin Evans
July 2017

1

WHAT'S TO APPRECIATE?

Shouldn't that be: "What's NOT to appreciate?"

Telegraph poles have long been a ubiquitous feature of the civilized landscape. Great lines of poles traversing the country in all directions. Carrying endless strands of copper wire off into perspective infinity, delivering morse code sparks at first, then analogue voice signals and ultimately internet broadband. As communication technology advanced, their stature, complexity and visibility were reduced. Wires that could once only carry a single telephone conversation can now multiplex hundreds of complaints to Channel Four - all at the same time. With the advent of hypertext transfer protocols these same wires can also deliver endless facebook posts about hilarious cat antics or photos of the sausage & mash lunch at the White Horse.

The telephone poles our landscape once knew are fast becoming a relic. Enormous multi-armed pole structures with dozens of cables strung between them being replaced by vanilla straight poles and a single wire. These are so lacking in character that it cannot be a surprise that we no longer notice them. Appreciating poles, is part admiration for the lines that they form in the countryside, or sillhouette they make against a rural skyline but also the historic preservation of what is really an industrial artefact.

The true pole aesthete wouldn't, nay couldn't, ignore electricity distribution poles either. After all these are still tall wooden structures with cabling and insulators - albeit glass rather than ceramic. But the aesthetic effect is almost the same.

On the next page, veteran connoisseur Willie Montgomery Stack, provides a short essay on the history of telegraph pole appreciation. Mr Stack began preparing said essay some years ago whilst chair of the East Dorset TPAS - an unhappy time he says, given the police enquiry and all those wasteful and inconclusive prosecutions. Nonetheless said essay aims to examine the origins of appreciating, some of the leading figures in the field, its growing importance in both scientific and artistic terms and its gradual evolution right up to the formation of TPAS itself.

Telegraph Pole Appreciation
by W.M. Stack

The appreciation of the telegraph pole as an object of beauty,
nay veneration, is first to be seen in the works of the social
thinker and art critic John Ruskin (1819–1900). The arrival
of telegraph poles – on the Great Western Railway in 1837
– coincided with Ruskin's redefining of art criticism:
combining polemic with aesthetics, scientific observation and
ethics. Hence, his rebuke to his friend JWM Turner on seeing
the artist's great work Rain, Steam and Speed, depicting a GWR
engine passing Maidenhead bridge: "Nice enough, Joey boy, but
why the bloody hell did you leave out all the lovely poles?"

Around this time, Ruskin became acquainted with William
Wordsworth and it is believed to have been Ruskin's persuasion
that led the elderly Wordsworth to update an earlier poem:

> I wandered lonely as a cloud
> That floats on high o'er vales and hills,
> When all at once I saw a crowd,
> A host, of gorgeous telegraph poles;

(The original version is now almost completely forgotten. It
mentioned something about snapdragons.)

The newly-appearing telegraph poles had struck a chord with
Ruskin. Dr Urma Gamble has suggested in her biography of
Ruskin that they may have reminded him of the gondola poles on
the Grand Canal in Venice. But could there have been a deeper,
darker association? In a letter to his old Oxford tutor, the
Revd Osborne Gordon, Ruskin wrote: "I'd rather be staring at
one of those things all covered with wires than looking at my
wife's lady bits." Mrs Effie Ruskin (nee Gray) was later to have
their marriage annulled for non-consummation.

Willie Montgomery Stack

THE SEMAPHORE TOWER APPRECIATION SOCIETY

present

WHIST DRIVE

to be held in the

CHURCH HUT

Friday, 19TH Oct

Large Prizes

Sack of coal, Woollen toilet roll dolly, Bath oil,
Tin of pear halves, Book of prayers, 2 rabbits.

Cards... 1/7½d

published by messrs blohm und voss gmbh, hamburg, deutschland

In the beginning the earth was formless and empty, darkness was over the surface of the deep.

Then there was a long middle bit with hardly any telegraph poles at all until Michael Faraday came along to make some sparks with a coil of wire and this gave people ideas.

Simultaneously a network of 30 ft wooden "notice board" poles had been erected around the country as a means of disseminating information via A4 sized posters pinned at head height. This superseded the long-established method of telling the lady in the post office queue.

English inventors Sir William Fothergill Cooke and Charles Wheatstone had been experimenting with spark-plug transmission and went on to patent a 5 needle device for signalling a 13 mile stretch of the Great Western Railway from Paddington station. The cables for this were buried the entire length in a steel conduit.

One day, out for a walk, William Cooke - I don't think he was a Sir at this point - came upon a notice pertaining to a forthcoming Whist Drive on one of these "notice" poles when he chanced up and marvelled at its great height. That was when he had his breakthrough idea of stringing these "telegraph" wires between them instead of labouriously burying them each time. The age of the telegraph pole was upon us.

Charles Wheatstone

There were further developments in the technology and reliability to ensure a furiously paced propagation of the network across the country – all on vast runs of these all-new telegraph poles.

Sir Benjamin Spoon BEM

Sir Benjamin Spoon B.E.M. had until that time dedicated his life to the admiration of semaphore towers which dotted the country. These were basically tall arm-waving devices attached to the top of domed buildings in order to send messages via flag semaphore over modest distances.

When the new fangled "telegraph" poles started to take over from the incumbent towers Sir Benjamin began to admire them instead. As they became all-pervasive he began to appreciate them, and ultimately to *really* appreciate them. On 9th October 1853 his seven member Semaphore Tower Appreciation Society voted in a special general meeting to henceforth ignore semaphore towers and to appreciate tall wooden, sticky-uppy poles with wires coming out the top instead. The Telegraph Pole Appreciation Society was born.

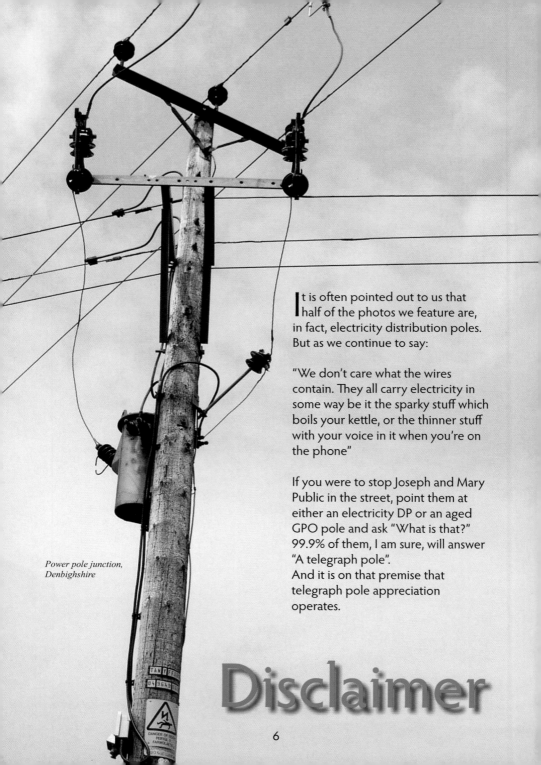

Power pole junction,
Denbighshire

It is often pointed out to us that half of the photos we feature are, in fact, electricity distribution poles. But as we continue to say:

"We don't care what the wires contain. They all carry electricity in some way be it the sparky stuff which boils your kettle, or the thinner stuff with your voice in it when you're on the phone"

If you were to stop Joseph and Mary Public in the street, point them at either an electricity DP or an aged GPO pole and ask "What is that?" 99.9% of them, I am sure, will answer "A telegraph pole".
And it is on that premise that telegraph pole appreciation operates.

Disclaimer

*Ever decaying phone-box
and accompanying pole
Abergwesyn, Powys*

All wire-carrying wooden poles, as far as me,
this book, and our society are concerned,
have an essence of whimsical poetry all of
their own. There they stand, silent sentinels,
forever observing us who scurry about
beneath them, oblivious.
Our society mantra is:

**"If it's tall, wooden, sticky-uppy and got
wires coming out the top then it gets
appreciated"..**

THE WONDER of the AGE ! !

INSTANTANEOUS COMMUNICATION.

Under the special Patronage of Her Majesty & H.R.H. Prince Albert.

THE GALVANIC AND ELECTRO-MAGNETIC

TELEGRAPHS,

ON THE

GT. WESTERN RAILWAY.

May be seen in constant operation, daily, (Sundays excepted) from 9 till 8, at the

TELEGRAPH OFFICE, LONDON TERMINUS, PADDINGTON AND TELEGRAPH COTTAGE, SLOUGH STATION.

An Exhibition admitted by its numerous Visitors to be the most interesting, and ATTRACTIVE of any in this great Metropolis. In the list of visitors are the illustrious names of several of the Crowned Heads of Europe, and nearly the whole of the Nobility of England.

"*This Exhibition, which has so much excited Public attention of late, is well worthy a visit from all who love to see the wonders of science.*"—MORNING POST.

The Electric Telegraph is unlimited in the nature and extent of its communications; by its extraordinary agency a person in London could converse with another at New York, or at any other place however distant, as easily and nearly as rapidly as if both parties were in the same room. Questions proposed by Visitors will be asked by means of this Apparatus, and answers thereto will instantaneously be returned by a person 20 Miles off, who will also, at their request, ring a bell or fire a cannon, in an incredibly short space of time, after the signal for his doing so has been given.

The Electric Fluid travels at the rate of 280,000 Miles per Second.

By its powerful agency Murderers have been apprehended, (as in the late case of Tawell,)—Thieves detected; and lastly, which is of no little importance, the timely assistance of Medical aid has been procured in cases which otherwise would have proved fatal.

The great national importance of this wonderful invention is so well known that any further allusion here to its merits would be superfluous.

N.B. Despatches sent to and fro with the most confiding secrecy. Messengers in constant attendance, so that communications received by Telegraph, would be forwarded, if required, to any part of London, Windsor, Eton, &c.

ADMISSION ONE SHILLING.

T. HOME. *Lie*

Nurton, Printer, 48, Church St. Portman Market.

Courtesy BT Heritage & Archives

USE BLOCK LETTERS FOR TELEGRAMS

STAN KROL

Courtesy BT Heritage & Archives

PRINTED BY H.M. STATIONERY OFFICE PRESS, TILEYARD ROAD, N.7. 3591

P.R.D. 563

ALIGNMENT

alignment
/əˈlʌɪnm(ə)nt/
noun:

arrangement in a straight line or in
correct relative positions.

It is no real surprise to me that telegraph poles may be a source of endless fascination to those who find themselves anywhere along the autism spectrum. The miles of connected poles, their intriguing symmetry and the shape they make in the landscape as they vanish into perspective infinty across endless hedges and distant treelines.

To one of our members - who we shall call agent #0650 – they are as a line of dancers holding hands across the fields. "A pig in mud", his mum said as she told me that the two of them have spent many a happy hour following the lines of poles "dancing" across the countryside, pausing to gaze up into their dizzying, towering form, quickly noting the credentials and off to the next one. So, not just me then...

The true appreciator of telegraph poles totally gets the aesthetic qualities of poles protruding as tall flowers from our landscape.

The Isle of Mull, Argyll & Bute, is where NASA sends prospective astronauts to ride the bus service between Tobermory and Calgary. It turns out that the G forces experienced on this route far exceed their own purpose-built centrifuges.

The Isle of Mull is also where you can still find lines of poles like these, captured by experienced telegraphpoleologist, John Cranston. The words "simply" and "gorgeous" spring to mind. The pole that is, not necessarily John Cranston.

photo © Len Gao aka peace-on-earth.org

The Kalmyk steppe in Russia. Vast enough to break the spirit of invading Wehmacht forces. But with lines of poles like these enough to raise the spirit of die-hard telegraph pole connoisseurs and move this place up three places to #6 in my all-time top places to go before I die*. Not half.

* #1 is National Lottery HQ to pick up a winners' cheque.

Graeme Fisher took a day trip to the Cable & Wireless Telegraph Museum, Porthcurno. This sounds like it should be in Wales but is, in fact, Cornwall. The longest run of the shortest poles anywhere in the world.

Taking power to the Hinterland aka "y Gwyll" - as we watched it in Wales
- these high-power line-dancers running juice from the Hydro scheme at
Cwmrheidol (where I live) over the murderous, sombre badlands beyond.

I was once employed as pub pianist in the White Lion (Llew Gwyn) near Aberystwyth. It was my job to abruptly stop playing the moment a stranger came into the bar. And if it was an Englishman we all had to start talking Welsh. Those who couldn't speak Welsh had to just make something up. It's true is that.

Frome-based academic ceramic addict, Jake Rideout provided
this POTM for March 2016.
"This pole is unusual", he says, "as it is a double pole and carries
six 33,000v lines which split apart into two separate pole routes
about a mile up the line. " And it looks nice too.

Every village should be like Quorn in Leicestershire - that is to have a proprietory brand of vegan fungal protein named after them. Not only that but to also have its own brilliant online digital museum that runs to thousands of pages as an excellent on-line resource.

Sue Templeman of said museum wrote and asked me something technical about the poles in this picture. Alas, I was unable to help her. What she should have asked was "don't you think these poles are lovely?" Yes, Sue, they really are I would have replied. www.quornmuseum.com

LOUGHBORO' RD. QUORN

It's less the alignment and more the loneliness and isolation of these Icelandic high voltage distribution poles that appeals. Plus the fact that it was taken by somebody called Hâfi Martsindottir who had just spent 14 days living in the back of a Skoda Favia with her Russian boyfriend - in winter. Bathing in the hot pools and surviving on the local delicacy: Pottur núðla.
Rumours of a familial connection to Ms Martinsdottir are not unfounded.

Our aforementioned agent #0650 clearly has an eye finely tuned for aligned poles. His primary passion is for power distribution, but these float our boat for sure. Don't ask where they are. Let's say Somerset.

More island-hopping. Hebridean power poles to infinity and beyond on Tiree. Most folk visit Tiree for the wind-surfing. We visit for the windswept poles. And the rain. And, of course, the soup at the airport cafe.

This line of poles along a country lane in Donegal captures the divine essence of pole appreciation. Uncomplicated poles in a simple landscape taking the eye, the fancy and the thin electric voices within the copper cores on their merry way towards Malin at the very top of Ireland.
I'll get my coat.

So when is a pole too much?
Somehow, this 1935 photo of a run of poles over
Bucktone Moor, just transgresses beyond elegance
and into the realms of industrial. Individually each
is a handsome pole but the sum of the parts equals
a vista-hogging whole.

photo courtesy of BT Heritage & Archives

21

Founder

Born on board a steamship during a perilous crossing of the River Gwenfro in 1802, Benjamin Spoon, found notoriety fairly late in life.

Until his "Grand Idea" of putting cheese together with onion in the form of a thin slice of fried potato, he had struggled to make ends meet as a small time inventor. This "Eureka" moment took place just after his carriage shed a wheel after hitting a Lucozade bottle on the modern day B5105 near what is today called Llanfihangel. That was in 1863.

His invention , which briefly became popular in Victorian society was said to be "sampled favourably" by her Majesty, Queen Victoria. Benjamin may have been more successful though had he called his product something more catchy than "sliced onion flavoured potato slivers with some cheese". Staying with the onion theme he also came up with the notion of making pickled onion flavoured corn starch snacks in the shape of strange beasts. Again, his nomenclature let him down and "slightly scary beast-shaped puffy corn snacks" never caught on.

Cheese & Onion crisps were re-invented in the 1950s by Irishman Joe Murphy who made his fortune with the Tayto crisp company. Monster Munch had to wait another hundred years before seeing the light of day.

Sir Benjamin enjoys a cigar on the touchline prior to the excitement of the game. Here with his gentleman assistant, Huw Thayer

Queen Victoria never forgot Benjamin's snacks though and he was remembered in her birthday honours with the Empire Medal in 1864 and the Sir bit the year after.

Sadly, Sir Benjamin Spoon BEM died penniless in 1870 after losing his fortune to a football pools betting scam.
He is buried in Cerrigydrudion churchyard.

Wrexham captain, Ashley Westwood, listens intently to tactical advice imparted by Sir Benjamin. Had they heeded said advice, the result would have been a resounding thrashing for the opponents.

Sir Benjamin cracks the first of many bottles of champagne. A defeat is only a victory backwards after all.

In March 2009 Sir Benjamin arose briefly from the dead to be guest of honour at a prestigious football event in the Blue Square Conference of Great British footy.

The game between Wrexham and Kidderminster Harriers was a must-win contest for both sides.

As it happened, those bounders from the West Midlands went home with all 3 vital points due to a 94th minute flapping of handbags in the Wrexham defence. Much jeering followed.

After the game, Sir Benjamin hung around the bar answering questions from bar staff regarding how much ice to put in his whiskey. He also took the opportunity to mingle with curious onlookers and to converse in a vaguely coherent manner. Then, as quickly as he arrived, he disassembled himself back to his Denbighshire graveyard where he's spent the last 150 years.

Sir Benjamin offers to clean man of the match, Andrew Crofts' shirt of all the felt-pen scrawling. Or rather, his manservant, Huw Thayer, will clean it. And in his own time too.

Stalinist era poster urging the proletariate on to ever greater telegraph pole appreciation in the great patriotic struggle against the bourgouise - and any one else Uncle Joe didn't like. Communist utopias don't just happen. circa 1933.

Hieroglyphs

T he observant citizen will look up to read the markings on every telegraph pole they pass, mentally noting the age, condition and size of each ready to transcribe to their notebooks once they get home. A normal person couldn't give a toss.
So considering that you've bought this book in the first instance must place you as an observing kind. So what do all these engravings, plaques and embossed badges mean?

• **This pole belongs to B.T.** *[1]

• The horizontal notch is the "doby" mark, i.e. 3m from the bottom of the pole and 1.2m from ground level. A complex process of arithmetical deduction leads us to the fact that this pole is planted in a hole 1.8m deep.

• It is 9 metres long and is categorised as a "Light" pole. Perm any 1 from Light, Medium, Stout.

• It was preserved (in creosote) in 2009. It will have been planted possibly years after that.

• The **3** refers to the depot whence the pole came - in this case Burt Boulton & Haywood Ltd (BBH), Newport, Gwent. The "**I**" denotes the species of tree "Imported European Redwood" namely Scots Pine/Pinus Sylvestris.

[1] As do 4 million BT poles in the UK.

Definitive pole suppliers and their codes. Score 1 point for each depot pole spotted. 6 points attains telegraph pole anorak status.
- · Depot 1 - James Jones (ceased supplying BT 1998)
- · Depot 2 - Calders & Grandidge (current supplier)
- · Depot 3 - BBH (current supplier)
- · Depot 4 - PTG (supplied BT between 1997-2000 taken over by Scanpole & moved production to the continent)
- · Depot 5 - Scanpole (supplied BT 2000-2006)
- · Depot 6 - Scanpole (supplied BT 2000-2006)

Special thanks to Graeme Donkin & Peter Gerrard for their wisdom here.

• **This pole belongs to the Post Office.**

• It is 8 metres long and is also categorised as a "Light" pole.

• It was preserved in 1970.

There is no doby mark and no pole depot identifier. And rarer to find the PO without a preceding G. I scored 7 points for myself in my own competition that I made up by me for myself by finding this pole.

GPO Pole

28 ft*[1] long Medium pole, preserved in 1937.

Regular ascender of telegraph poles, John Brunsden scores maximum marks for finding this one. But loses points because he had a head start over every one else. So I still win.

HCT pole

The People's Republic of Hull has a long history of doing things its own way with regards to electronic communication. Hull City Telephone Department (1882-1987) became Kingston Communications and was the UK's first all digital network in 1989. So, 3 points for spotting one of these poles, and probably 2 points for a new fangled KC or KCL pole. Thanks to Aaron Bailey for his Hull based eagle eye.

*[1] Seeing as we're talking old money, 28 ft is 1.69697 rods, 18.66 cubits, 0.0424242 furlongs.

Other adornments

This pole was not planted deep enough for whatever reason: hedge bank, rocky ground, it was Friday afternoon.

C = Shallow, climbable.

Decayed pole. Defective. Damaged, Deficient, Dodgy, Dunce. The precise definition of the 'D' pole has caused much debate in telegraph pole circles - this once culminated in an online squabble of such ferocity that the fire-service were called and the whole forum had to be hosed down to return the cyber-assembly to a normal operating temperature.

If there is a 'Z' plate on a pole it means there is a hazard next to the pole i.e. a spiked fence, a poorly cooked chicken breast or a Rt Hon Member for Uxbridge & South Ruislip. For a Z pole the engineer can still position his/her ladders in such a way as to reduce the hazard rendering it safe to climb.

H is for hazard. unlike a Z pole where the engineer could position their ladders to eliminate the hazard threat, the H pole can only be worked on through use of a hoist or other apparatus that begins with the letter H.
10 points if you find one of these.

Test cycle, see opposite for reasons why I don't know much about these.

Shallow planted pole, but climbable. If you're not scared of heights.

Basically, don't hang too many wires off this pole in any one direction - you'll only go and pull it over. 7 wires in this instance. I'm guessing here but I reckon a really big-boned pigeon could probably have this pole down.

A559 - Maximum Pole Loading

Do not exceed

⓪①②③④⑤⑥⑦⑧⑨⑩⑪⑫⑬⑭⑮
dropwire spans in any 180 degree arc

Refer to current instructions before adding or removing any aerial cables, stays or struts

D.P = Distribution Pole/ Point. Identified by the number 21 presumably so somebody can find it on a map or put it on a "to do" list. From this pole will run lines of sub poles to various properties.

I confess to never having completely got my head around these ones. Since 1964 telegraph poles have been affixed with a punched-hole testing cycle label. This one was last tested in August 2006, test cycle G. Or is it test cycle L. Another engineer tells me that this last row identifies the tester. What am I supposed to do? This book is about appreciating telegraph poles, not how to be an engineer so I'm going to leave this right here.*[1]

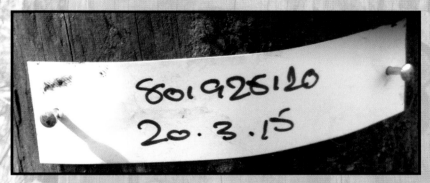

We live in viciously litigious times. Unless there is a highly conspicuous notice warning of the dangers of inserting appendages into hot fat someone is likely to lose the shirt off their back should you then choose to remove your freshly-cooked chips by hand. It is with this in the back of their minds that large, highly sueable, firms take risk-aversion to dizzying new heights.

Nowadays, before they climb a pole, telephone engineers have to thoroughly test said pole for climbability (I kid you not) and afix a label to prove that they have done so.

For the test itself, the engineer has to whack the pole with a hammer at least three quarters of the way around the base. They are listening for a ringing A# note, 4 octaves below middle C which indicates no decay. A label bearing the date and the engineer's ID has to be affixed using hammer and nails approx 4 inchs from the base.

Of course, this test then introduces the added risk of "cobbler's thumb" and other potential lawsuited injuries.

So, in the interests of rigorous Health & Safety (gone mad) our engineer must don safety harness, hi-viz, helmet, goggles, tipped boots AND get mummy or daddy to help him (or her) when using the hammer or any scissors or pointy things. You couldn't make it up!

*[1] Apparently it's the engineer's ID - GL in this case. Later ones have 4 letters. Fancy that!

Pole #31 on a run somewhere. These iron numbered nails, delightfully collectable, infuriatingly unremoveable seem to have been superceded by plastic tags. See previous page.

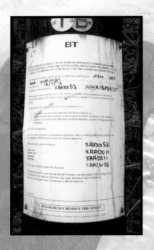

You'll see one of these posters on almost every new, heavily creosoted pole that BT and their contractors puts up.

This, apparently, is your notice of right to object to overhead apparatus under paragraph 17 of the electronics communications code, telecommunications act 1984 schedule 2 blah drone waffle.

Truth is that nobody really knows what they're for as not a single person ever has ever read one to the end. Lower down - if you read it fully - you'll find a treatise on the development of progressive rock as an art form.

The A1024 is a 1.4 mile long relief road for traffic wishing to avoid Norwich city centre. This seems bonkers to me because I always manage to avoid Norwich city centre by staying in Wales.

A1024 is also a notice BT put on poles to say it needs replacing. Why couldn't they just say that then?

You can claim 6 points for finding one of these rarities. David Kendrick (#0609H) did.

Cobra was a means of prolonging a pole's life by injecting an arsenic-based preservative via a syringe at the vulnerable ground level point (where moisture and oxygen encourage the growth of rot).

One set of markings you are never likely to see - that is the pole inspector's initials at the bottom of each pole. Pole inspectors, select and inspect growing crops of woodland throughout UK and also Scandinavia, the Baltic states and Russia.

Worthy of a book all of its own, I'm sure, but here I just want to point out the intials W.M. in faded paint. W..M. probably stands for William McGrory. Or maybe Walter Mitty, or Wendy Middlemarch. These are my suggestions, feel free to make up your own.

The Great COVER UP

Conspiracy theories? We love 'em.
   Flat earth, Aliens in the Whitehouse, Prince-Charles-the-lizard-king sort of thing. And I know for a fact that Neil Armstrong was playing golf in Hawaii on the day he was supposed to be walking on the moon.

   We'd long suspected that telecom contractors had been concealing telegraph poles around the country - for nefarious reasons. We felt the world needed to know and so sent TPAS Special Agent #0484H Adrian Trainsett undercover to find out. And the pictures he brought back are as shocking and damning as they are as poor quality.

08:55am

   A Telecoms inspector arrives from a well-known British Telecoms company. The photos are low quality due to having been taken through Agent Trainsett's vest.

09:25am

   After a refreshing cup of tea in the aforementioned Telecom company's van and a read of the Daily Star, said inspector climbs the ladder and attaches a bundle of foliage to the top.

10:47am

   Two more tea-breaks, a quick look at the sudoku, another fag and then back up the pole to nail up more tree stuff.

   Truck load of foliage can be seen waiting to be attached.

11:55am

They're nothing if not meticulous. More tea, a nip off to the shop for some pasties and a twix then back to the job in hand.

The foliage has to be fitted properly otherwise it won't look convincing.

1:22pm

Very little left to see of the original pole. A whole skip load of foliage has been attached to this pole and 18 cups of tea consumed.

2:37pm

The afternoon tea break is very short. They realise they've taken the mick a bit too far and they'll end up having to work over.
Just the finishing touches now though. Time for one more cup of tea, a fag, a biscuit and a quick shufty at that mag Terry brought before sodding off home.

3:22pm

That's it, job done! Hop back into the van, wedge all the crisp packets and pop-bottles under the seat for the next crew to deal with and drive off back to the depot.
Another telegraph pole covered over to spare the blushes of sensitive ladies who may be passing and aroused by such things.

F.A.Q.

How big are telegraph poles ?

No hard and fast answer. But 30ft (9m) would be a good average pole. They are classed for width as (L) Light, (M) Medium, (H) Heavy or the less commonly used Stout. And you can score 4 points every time you find an XL (Extra Light) pole.

How many are there?

About 4 million according to someone from BT that I spoke to. As for power distribution poles. No idea. Let's say 3,207,551 - a prime number too. Yes, that sounds good.

What are they made of?

Wood. *Come on, pay attention!* And the crossarms are also made of wood. A different type though - a tropical hardwood called kerruing.

How deep are they planted?

A pole should be "planted" approx 6ft (1.8m) into the ground.
The doby mark is a notch 3 metres from the bottom of the pole. A pole then correctly planted would show the 3 metre mark at a height of 1.2 metres above ground level.

How many are there?

I told you already - about 4 million.

How long does a telegraph pole last?

There is no reason why a properly treated pole shouldn't last 100 years. We know of one that was "planted" in 1908 and is still not even classed as decayed.

How many are there?

What's the matter with you? It's on page one of the flipping website!

How often are they tested?

They are tested first at 12 years from new then on a 10 year rolling cycle of inspection. The inspection is often scurrilously described as the pole being whacked with a hammer and the inspector listening for the dull thud of rot. However, proper inspection requires a sample boring from the ground line.

Who is responsible for telephone poles?

B.T. Openreach. NOT the Telegraph Pole Appreciation Society. We just admire them. So if a pole near you has fallen down, or something has dropped off one onto your car windscreen then it is nothing to do with us.

What about power distribution poles?

Your local power company. Around here (in Wales) it's Scottish Power. Presumably they have Welsh power in Scotland. Anyway, see previous answer pertaining to "nowt to do with us".

What does the red "D" plate mean?

This pole was found to be defective (likely decayed) at its last inspection. It is marked for replacement, as and when! A pole can be defective because:
A. It's rotten.
B. It's not planted deep enough.
C. It has too many wires hanging off it + insufficient stay wires to counter-balance.
D. Too close to spiked railings.
E. It has too many Coffee Morning posters stuck to it.

Are we nearly there yet?

Not far now.

Are the crossarms on a telegraph pole always on the side nearest London?

Yes, absolutely. Except for all those where they're not of course.

How much oil could a gum boil boil if a gum boil could boil oil?

The answer is a surprising 18.3 millilitres. Owing to relative density and fluid viscosity only 17.4 ml of water could be boiled in the same gum boil.

How many members does the Telegraph Pole Appreciation Society have?

We don't use standard member numbering, rather a terminal digit filing system together with a random element based on a "seed" generated from the radiation emitted from a pulsar in the Orion nebula. We then plug this resultant value in to the right side of a Friedmann equation and raise it to the power of the nearest prime. So roughly 700,000,000,000 nanomembers

Approximately how many telegraph poles are there.

Four fox hake! What the hell do you need to know that for anyway?

Dave Bennett

真正的革命者穿着漂亮的帽

Learn from Lei Feng Day

At this time of year the Zhengzhou branch of WH Smith is awash with greeting cards dedicated to and celebrating the life of Lei Feng.

This retailing frenzy culminates on March 5th, celebrated as "Learn from Lei Feng Day", when card recipients are urged to live their lives like Mr Feng.

Who hell he? I hear you ask. And what's he doing in this book?

Born of poor peasants in Hunan Province, in 1940, Lei Feng was brought up by the Communist party after his father was killed by the Japanese and his mother killed by herself. He then went on to join the People's Liberation Army, became a squad leader and a super-diligent member of the party.

Yes, but what's he doing here?

His study of the works of Chairman Mao taught him to live a life of extreme obedience, frugality, selflessness and devotion of his body and soul to the revolution - wanting nothing more than to be "a revolutionary screw that never rusts".

Will you please just get to the point!

He is a cultural icon, a beacon of altruism and a concentrated expression of communist ideals. All of which came to an end at the tender age of 22 years when he was killed by a telegraph pole. Yes, China's courageous guiding light, their moral exemplum, their Prince Edward, was squashed as his friend Qiao Anshan backed a truck into a telegraph pole which fell on to the poor chap's head.

Learn from Lei Feng - Beware, the lethal combination of reversing trucks, telegraph poles and feelings of impending fate.

Telegraph poles can kill! Be careful out there.

Commie icon Lei Feng (left). The caption translates as: "Real revolutionaries wear nice hats"

MURDER HE WROTE

The week all started routinely enough.

There I was busy appreciating the daily influx of photographs submitted by enthusiastic subscribers to our sagest of societies. including the finialed beauty you see below - which has the look of South Shropshire about it. They came from an email address in hotmail which ought to have raised suspicions, if not hackles. No note was attached.

Things took a turn for the sinister when we received the photograph (*right*) a day

later. From the same email address. And this time there was a note (*also right*).

We were struck with horror. Anybody who knows me would realise that if someone were to give me a penny, I still wouldn't have two pennies to rub together. So even if I did somehow know the whereabouts of an ageing water pump I could never put my hand on that kind of money. So we had to play the waiting game.

Then I noticed that the evil fiend had carelessly signed his name at the bottom and so I started to put two and two together.

My mate Pete Greenrod has a broken-down Vauxhall Cavalier in the scrap yard he calls his garden. He also has manky, stinking trainers like those in the picture. But then it couldn't be him - I'm sure his is the 1984 model Cavalier. And the ransom note specifically says that it's not him anyway, it's some other Pete. So a red herring then.

This story didn't have a happy ending, and appreciators of telegraph poles should skip a page now.

We received the final photograph (*bottom right*) subsequently. An act of vile desperation, carried out without compunction by a soulless Vauxhall (and Ryobi chainsaw) owner. Probably with a wood stove and who doesn't mind the stink of burning creosote.

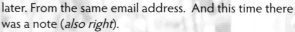
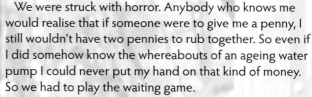

38

£100 And A
REPLACEMENT
WATER PUMP FOR
A 1983
VAUXHALL
CAVALIER

OR THE POLE
GETS IT

WE MEAN
BUSINESS

CHEERS   PETE
        NOT GREENROD, ANOTHER
                PETE

Visit
THE FABLED LOST POLE

of
Bala Leisure Centre
plus
Miracle tour of the
INCREDIBLE
VANISHING
Telegraph Poles
of the B5105

BALA   3¾
Pallet World   7¼
(B5105)

Canolfan
Hamdden
Leisure
Centre

Llyn
Lake

ISSUED BY:
GULLIBLE'S TRAVEL Ltd
123 TEGID ST. BALA. TELEPHONE BALA EXCHANGE 37.
ALL JOURNEYS START AND TERMINATE IN BALA. NEXT THE LEISURE CENTRE.

FACT SPOT

Telecom Eireann engineers have come up with a novel way of getting around the budget cuts within the Irish GPO - simply don't bother with the lower half of their telegraph poles. No hole to dig, only half the wood used and technically no need to pay the wayleave ground rent either. This photo taken along the R181 somewhere near Castleblayney in central Ireland. Pole of the Month Mar 2011.

NASA have never been forthcoming about the reasons they chose to send a 25% scale GPO telephone pole along with 3 astronauts aboard the Apollo 14 mission. The pole, etched GPO, 3L 71, was planted by mission commander Alan B Shephard just north of crater 113 in the Fra Mauro formation on his second EVA on Feb 6th 1971. The pole was never connected to any communications equipment and no documentation of this bizarre, not to say risky, experiment exists.

Apollo 14

Telegraph pole site
Crater 113

What it says on the label. And it's true. In that exact spot and on that inexact date - somewhere in the borders of Scotland - nothing at all happened. And, what's more, has continued, to this day, not to happen.

41

ARTY POLES

I have rattled on about the aesthetics of telegraph poles, if not forever then certainly ad-nauseum. But artists, proper ones, paint not just nudes or bowls of fruit but telegraph poles too. And why would they do that were they not the things of beauty I insist they are? Telegraph pole art is appreciation in concentrated form. The artist totally "gets" pole aesthetics and truth be this book needed only this single chapter to demonstrate the finer points of telegraph pole appreciation. But then it would just be a pamphlet and you wouldn't have this weighty tome kipped coquettishly on your coffee table for your guests to admire; I wouldn't make a small fortune from its enormous sales and my place as an author of greatness would be in question.

Anyway, pride of place in the boardroom at TPAS HQ - and just above our mantelpiece display of retired ceramic insulators - is an original painting called "#15 Mixed Media on canvas (100cm x 50cm)" by London based Joe Simpson.
This was from Joe's "Everything is Electrified" collection which included a number of pylon paintings too. See following pages for more.

#195 Mixed Media on Canvas. 100 x 50 cm. SOLD - TO US.

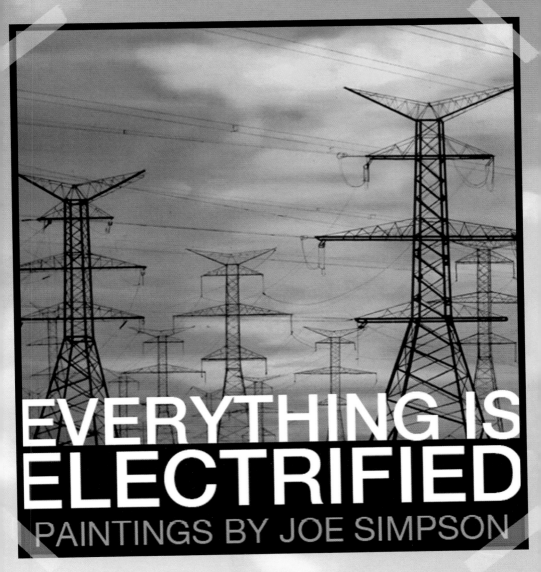

EVERYTHING IS
ELECTRIFIED
PAINTINGS BY JOE SIMPSON

www.joe-simpson.co.uk

#18 Mixed Media on Canvas.
25 x 25 cm.
SOLD

www.joe-simpson.co.uk

#19 Mixed Media on Canvas.
25 x 25 cm.
SOLD

www.joe-simpson.co.uk

45

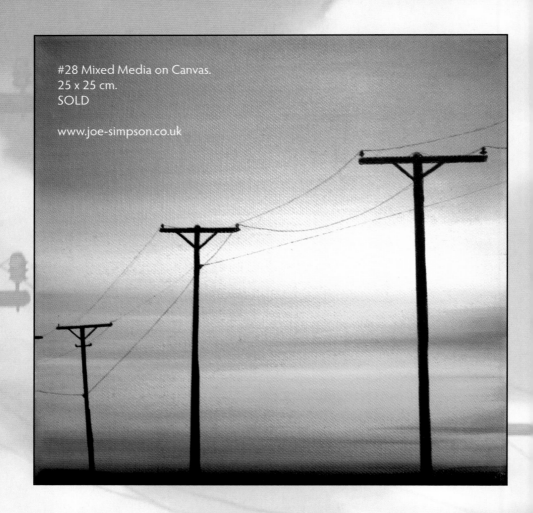

#28 Mixed Media on Canvas.
25 x 25 cm.
SOLD

www.joe-simpson.co.uk

#22 Mixed Media on Canvas.
50 x 20 cm.
SOLD

www.joe-simpson.co.uk

#24 Mixed Media on Canvas.
50 x 20 cm.
SOLD

www.joe-simpson.co.uk

Ok, so now we know, Joe Simpson can totally capture the jizz of telegraph poles. And these paintings are all sold so we conclude that the art-buying public appreciate poles too. We're thinking of starting an internet pressure group to try to persuade Joe to do some more.

#paintsomemoretelegraphpolespleasejoe

#30 Mixed Media on Canvas.
SOLD, I think
www.joe-simpson.co.uk

Tamsin Pastelle

Out of the blue one day we received an email from **Simon Carter**, the curator of the Tamsin Pastelle museum and gallery, Salisbury, Wilts. His email contained a lost telegraphic masterpiece by said artist and in its original JPEG form too.

"This still-life in chalks by Tamsin Pastelle, entitled 'Insulators #1', (right) formed the central panel of a Triptych and is thought to have graced the South Entrance of the B.T. Chapel of Remembrance in Salisbury, Wiltshire.

Believed originally to have spent her formative years in the Southern Heavy Water Region of Britain, she was most active in the Reclamation Period. She discovered her passion for Telegraphics when annotating Satellites through a pin-hole; but for years had to work undetected for fear of her public persona, as resident floral artist (watercolours) at the tiny village of Christmas-in-the-Cotswolds, being publicly trashed. Had she not taken refuge 'neath a Rural Transformer on that day of providence..."

Extract taken from art notes compiled for the Tamsin Pastelle Memorial Gallery of Street Furniture.

Simon eluded to further artwork finds by this great telegraph pole artist. Herewith the first.

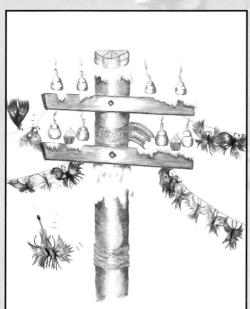

Tamsin's cake and butterfly period (possibly) followed a poorly-judged fungal foray which led to a plate of garlic magic-mushrooms on toast. She may have ended up with a gippy stomach and an interesting insight, but we mortals have this colourful, vibrant, psilocybin-induced candle and butterfly filled masterpiece to remember her by.

This and other paintings by the same artist can be bought in greetings card form from the US website cardgnome.com

Insulators #1
Tamsin Pastelle
Chalk

The Art Rooms

Jacky Al-Samarraie is the founder and sole creative force behind The Art Rooms (www.theartrooms.co.uk). Her characteristic style of simple sillhouettes and vibrant blocks of colour lends itself perfectly to picking out telegraph poles as punctuation in a rural landscape.

Leeds - Yeadon
Printed on 300gsm matt card 152 x 105mm

Beverley
152 x 105mm

I first came across these images as greetings cards and I liked them so much that they remain in their cellophane, unsent, as I can't bear to part with them.

www.theartrooms.co.uk

Dumfries & Galloway
152 x 105mm

Troutbeck
152 x 105mm

Tim Doyle

Tim Doyle grew up in the suburban sprawl of Dallas, Tx. Therein he turned inward and sullen, finding joy in comic-books and television. He moved to Austin, Texas in 1999 to fulfill a life-long dream of not living in Dallas.
He works as a print-maker and illustrator in a house full of cats.

Night falls on the SNPP, Tim Doyle

He describes himself as an appreciator of Telephone Poles and sundry electrical grid stuffs. This we get from these two re-imagined Simpsons inspired images from his "Unreal Estate" series. Also, contact Tim if you'd like a free cat.
Visit www.mrdoyle.com

Richard Kaye
Industrial & Urban Prints

Richard Kaye is an artist and print-maker from a particularly beautiful part of Devon. His chosen subjects tend towards figurative.

"Sometimes I become fascinated by certain objects such as animal skulls or driftwood, which have both been past fixations, much to the amusement of my friends!

"At the moment drypoint intaglio printmaking is my medium, and bold silhouettes my subject. Thus far I have started four series of prints. Those being: Telegraph Poles, Trees, Scaffolding and Communications Masts.

"I am fascinated with both printmaking and also silhouettes of things which people may not always consider to be artistic. Such as Telegraph Poles, Cranes and Communication Masts. I feel these can be really beautiful once composed in the right way. I also like the fact that they are modern and slightly edgy as a subject, yet portrayed using one of the most traditional and technical forms of printmaking. Drypoint intaglio.

"With Drypoint, I have to scratch the image reversed into a copper plate, then rub ink into the plate, remove the excess and finally print onto damp paper through an intaglio press. Each print plate is hand made and every print pulled by me in a studio in Devon UK."

www.etsy.com/uk/shop/RichardKayeArt

1/50   TELEGRAPH POLE VI   R Kaye

2/50   TELEGRAPH POLE II.   P.Kaye.

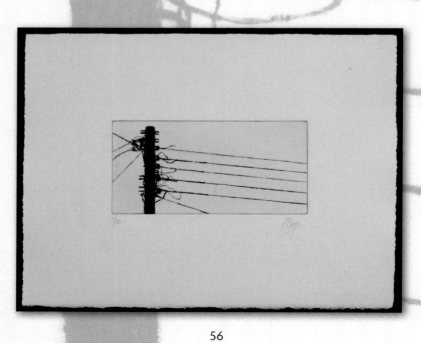

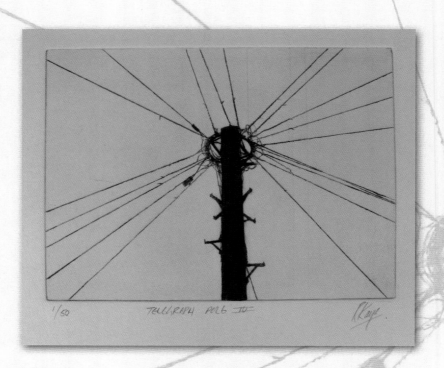

1/50   TELEGRAPH POLE IV   R Kaye

1/50   TELEGRAPH POLE I   E.Kaye.

Jo Burlington

Bridport-based Jo picks up the rather more utilitarian aesthetic of poles. She says, "I do enjoy the almost constant presence of the telegraph/utility poles and electricity transformers, substations and pylons and their wires like minimalist drawings everywhere.

I really don't understand how they work though... but that's part of what I like about

A Messy Romanian Utility Pole 100 x 150cm - Jo Burlington, 2017

them, they look like you should be able to understand them just by looking hard enough... but I cant, so what they do is magical.

I can imagine people worshiping them in some post-apocalyptic future and this is why I like to make these drawings, like homages. "

Jo's website www.joburlington.co.uk should be ready by the time you read this.

Utility Pole - Jo Burlington,

The Post Office

Overhead cable route through a country scene
Publicity poster with no text
Raymond Coxon, 1936

BT Heritage & Archives

Eric Ravilious 1903 - 1942

Wiltshire Landscape, pencil and watercolour, 1937.

   The 1930s was the great age of the motor car and touring the open road was almost
mandatory for the vehicle owning classes. This idealised vision of the countryside was
promoted by motoring organisations and any number of guide-books. Despite not being
a driver himself, Eric found inspiration in this landscape. His paintings have a soft almost
dreamlike quality and it is this undulating countryside with its endless lonely lane and line of
poles that I find so endearing. Apparently, Eric only added the van at a later point having
seen it in a Post Office magazine.
   Captain Eric Ravilious served as a war artist but was killed at the age of 39 whilst aboard a
Lockheed Hudson of RAF 269 squadron on a search and rescue mission off Iceland.
This painting, lot #129, going, going, went for £242,500 at Christie's, London in June 2014.

Polestar roundabout, Letterkenny (*Leitir Ceanainn*) Co. Donegal. This piece of public art by Derry artist Locky Morris - who never once played for the Undertones - cost €100,000 to make. I would have done it for €95,000 but there you go, Locky got in there first.

12 metres tall comprising 104 timber poles. The Polestar - the blurb says - alludes to the outline of a boat and something to do with rail and road and transport or something. Art blurb is notorious for its bollocks and I think I must have drifted off. Anyway, it is a cracking structure but I think if I'd got the gig I'd have put crossarms on the poles and a few insulators and wires all coming out the top.

The Poets...

It stands to reason that poets would be as touched by telegraph polar aesthetics as, say, me. When Current Archaeology magazine published an article about our most venerable of societies back in 2015 poet Margaret Seymour found inspiration. Her poem, reproduced here by kind permission, won first prize at the Sheringham poetry competition. So thanks to our ramblings, a myriad insulators, and the intrinsic beauty that is telegraph poles, these 152 words were selected out of all the thousands that are available and were assembled into the beautiful and unique, prize-lifting order that you see below. Congratulations and special thanks to Margaret. I've illustrated the whole occasion with a 1933 photo from BT Archives of a telegraph 'H' pole line at Tottenham.

Distance Writing

The telegraphpoleappreciationsocietydotorg
knows poetry when it sees it - the epic
march of metre, neat crossbar rhyme-schemes
embellished with ceramic references
to fungi, daleks, Chinese lanterns;
long lilting lines punctuated by swallows.

It's fond of folklore such as crossbars
are always on the side facing London.
It loves the drama of the telegram,
whistle and crackle of the human voice.
urgent pitter-pat of Morse,
the arcane doings of Openreach.

Its totems are the trunks of trees -
wayside gods inscribed with tribal marks
BT or GPO, plus date of last libation
of creosote. She of the high and shaky
brackets orders DO NOT CLIMB.
He of the yellow skull warns DANGER OF DEATH.

Happy the members of TPAS! For them
a road or railway is a procession
of curiosities, a document, a refuge
where ivy flourishes and kestrels perch,
a photographic pilgrimage where finally
lines of posts are enshrined as posts online.

Margaret Seymour

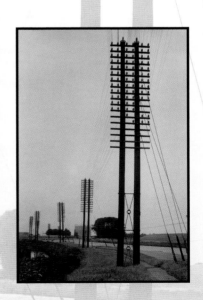

Lacoste in the Provence region in the south of France is famous for two things. One being its once notorious resident, **Donatien Alphonse Francois comte de Sade** aka the Marquis de Sade who had, shall we say, a peculiar attitude to familial relationships. The second thing Lacoste is famous for is its resident poet laureate – an Irish born poet-gardener by the name of **Finnbar Mac Eoin**. Finn, the author of "Two suitcases and a dog" has had a few run-ins himself with the rather parochial villagers. A quick search of his name using a well known search engine should lead you to the full story.

Anyway, poet that he is, Finn finds himself inspired by telegraph poles and submitted this poem to the only place he could or indeed should. And he kindly allowed us to pubish it. The poem is best read in a Co. Cork accent. Trust me.

Poles Apart.

In the forest they grew up
together side by side,
branches touching, all
resisting the Atlantic winds.

But now, they don't even
want to know each other,
totally individual and the
way they are cropped;

No foliage, not even a
limb for a bird to perch
on, anaemic looking, as
if they were anorexic.

It's all about the look, bare
legs and those porcelain
earrings that look hideous,
homogenous, no character.

In my day we all knew each
other, helped our neighbors.
Now, they're too weak to stand,
but for the wires! We're poles apart.

Finn Mac Eoin

And what about insulators? Don't they deserve a poem? Yes they do. And what's the chances of that - I just put my hand in to my desk drawer and what should I pull out? That's right, a biro with the ink all run out of it and stuck solid to a rubber. But after that? Yes, a poem about an insulator. One which was written for a found-object art installation at Ludlow Library a couple of years ago. Someone found an insulator, handed it in and a poet of complete unrenown wrote this rather moving poem about it. We all cried.

Insulator

Were you listening
all those years
atop the pole
between big house and the exchange?

What might you have heard
as those long dead voices whispered by?
Stockmarket talk,
household gossip,
inevitable war.

Your eavesdrop over
the telegraph done.
Crackling whispers you once carried
now take the high road.
And your secrets safe on
a shelf in the collector's home.

Martin Evans

Of course, I expect now you're asking "Where's the song section? Where's the bit about telegraph pole songs? Where's Glen Campbell's Wichita Lineman?" Well that is our anthem after all - we sing it before, during and after all our executive Society meetings. Alas our budget for this book wouldn't run to being able to reproduce that classic song here. So I'll hum it for you to avoid any copyright issues. One, two, one two three four...

I am a lineman for the doo doooo. Hmmm hmmm hmm hmm hmmm hmm hmm.
.....
Something something ..still on the Line. da da da dada dada dah...

An everyday tale of telegraph pole testers

The fate of a redundant Scottish Power distibution pole just outside Penrhyncoch lay in the balance. BT Openreach despatched veteran pole tester Ben Wells and his YTS sidekick Brad - who also happens to be his brother - to check it over with a view to commandeering for telephone use. Failure for the pole would mean the log pile or the pulping yard or, at best, a gate post.

First Brad, possessor of the shorter of the two straws had to dig around the base of the pole. Preliminary whack with a hammer and that elusive low A# note was faint but nonetheless there. Next, Ben with his considerably longer straw gets to play with the toys and fetched the really big one out from the van - the pole resistance tester. Now I have a background in electronics and it seems fair enough to me that this machine-gun like gadget would just test the electrical resistance of the pole interior thus determining the amount of moisture penetration. Not a bit of it. See test results on opposite page.

Pressed against the side of the pole, a flat-tipped needle protrudes and is forced into and right through the pole, parting the wood fibres as it goes, all the time measuring the resistant force from the wood itself. The wood fibres just close over again upon extraction completely without harm.

All the readings are within parameters, so 2 out of 2 so far. Ben then went through his mental checklist of Health & Safety satisfiers and donned or attached pretty much every litigation deflection device known in order to ascend the pole for the final check - another whack with the hammer at the top. This pole had been cut off square which normally would require it to be "D" plated - ie. defective.

Ben was happy there was plenty of life left in the now renamed telegraph pole DP11. All remnants of it's power distribution past were removed and BT ownership firmly declared by tester codename ABGL (see punch holes on the label).

**** RESULTS ****
LOVELY POLE IS THAT
YOU SHOULD HANG ON TO IT

DP
11

NOW
PROPERTY
OF
BT

Brad & Ben the telegraph pole men

TEST EACH POLE

BEFORE

CLIMBING

Stan Krol designed many posters for the GPO and other companies incl. London Transport, BOAC and even ROSPA - the accident people.
This, though, one of his classics from 1948.

BT Heritage & Archives

IT MAY BE DECAYED

READ R.G.41 PAGE 3

Cornwall...

As viewed through a hole in a pole from West Stowford, Devon. Drilled by society member #0469, John Brunsden. John spends his working day at an altitude of approximately 10 metres above ground level. With a proper footed ladder, guy ropes, hard hat, high viz, crampons and butty box it's a wonder he has the strength to get up there. Anyway whilst atop the ladder he does get time to ponder the wonders of the universe, the meaning of life and what is on the other side of that pole.

MISSING CAT

Have you seen Ralph? Missing since Friday. Last
seen eating something out of a bin top of Vale St.
He doesn't answer to any name though - he's a cat.
Always hungry. Meaows a lot.
Tel:

PLEASE

BE A RESPONSIBLE DOG OWNER AND PICK UP AND TAKE IT HOME THANKYOU.

Circus Mondao pitched up with their wagons into the edge of Aberystwyth this summer where they formed a defensive circle. Then they pushed all their trucks over sideways to create an impenetrable shield from where they poured a rain of discount flyers over the parapet and into any passers-by venturing within range.

Bus shelters, telegraph poles, car-windscreens all fell under this blitzkrieg barrage of fly-posting. The good people of this Cardigan Bay resort at first appeared to be holding out under this intense marketing siege. But in the end the two shows daily and Sunday matinee proved decisive and much circus merriment was had by all. Probably.

Apparently, you can come face-to-face with Jesus at Knucklas Baptist chapel according to this telegraph pole. Actually, if I were to come face to face with Jesus I think the first thing I would say is, in fact, "Jesus!"

Frankly it's a big claim for a chapel in, quite literally, the middle of nowhere.

This poster is going to be around a while though. Full lamination and 11 drawing pins. 2 in the bottom left corner and 3 of them with plastic covered heads. But, again, full marks to me for observation. I had an hour to kill and the Castle Inn didn't open until 6:30.

This sign was correct. There were indeed no windfarms anywhere near this pole in Cefn Coch, Montgomeryshire. The sign later found itself to be perpetuating a terrible untruth as it continued to declare "No Windfarms" whilst the landscape around it slowly saturated with the bloody things.

Not designed for longevity, this sign attached with a single nail and flapped around a lot in the wind.

Holidays for dogs! Whatever next. They very waggishly call themselves "Barking mad".

Barking mad! I am, I love the place. Ba-doom.... tish! Credit to someone else for that highly repeatable but increasingly lame joke.

Meanwhile, 3 points for the thin lamination. A further 3 points for rounding off the corners - nice touch that. But lose a point for low quality of the stapling in the top left hand corner. Though they have put it up perpendicular to earth and ignored the slant of the pole itself a 9m Medium pole preserved in 2009.

A World Without Telegraph Poles

Telegraph poles are so ubiquitous that non-anoraks ({n} a-norakic) are virtually blind to them. Just like you no longer notice that your computer hates you, that pop-music is just getting crapper or that Curly Wurlys are no longer as big as a window cleaner's ladder.

They might just be dull sticks with wires on to you, but what if they were all to disappear overnight? You might put your hat on to go out and fetch your paper from the corner shop when a sense of oddness would come over you. Puzzling. Something is different, not quite right. You probably wouldn't be able to put your finger on it at first.

In the interests of research for this book, we visited Cerrigydrudion- a village noted for its [*insert something positive here if you can think of anything. At all*] - in Conwy county, North Wales. We took the photograph you see at top, right. Then we popped over to an alternative universe where electricity had never been invented to have a look for ourselves.

Picture 1 (top). Our Universe, Cerrigydrudion High Street where telegraph poles flourish in total biodiversity. (N.B. In this universe Wrexham are an under-performing non-league, football team)

Picture 2 (bottom). Cerrigydrudion in a parallel universe where Wrexham are 4 times Champions of Europe but there isn't a pole to be seen. Anywhere. Tall, wooden, sticky-uppy things with wires coming out the top were never invented. What an even duller world than the one we just left.

Apart from the football differences, I think I prefer our universe version of Cerrigydrudion with all its aerial clutter and its very poor TV reception. While we were over there, we popped into the parallel White Lion and had a shock when the bar lady asked us for 1,550 Euros for an Evanly pint of Foyle's Gold.

Blatant product placement

W e can't quite run to the £27,000,000 that Danny Boyle blew on the 2012 olympic opening ceremony. But we do have a Roman Candle left over from last year and I think there's a pack of sparklers under the stairs somewhere. Yes,

21st September
is
Telegraph Pole
Appreciation Day

T his is the day when we finally look up and notice these tall, elegant and dignified keepers of the volts; be they telephone or electricity volts. All year long, and all weathers they perform their duty unflinching - holding aloft the wires carrying your telephone calls to your cousin who's just got engaged; or keeping up the cables delivering the electricity that makes your slim-o-matic adjustable vibrating tv lounger work. All in a day's work for a telegraph pole.[*1] So get outside and,

- hug a telegraph pole
- take a photgraph of one
- climb one
- write a poem about one
- admire one

Why not organise your own little celebration underneath your local pole? Maybe have a mini one-person street party with bunting and butterfly cakes and a bottle of pop with a wasp in it. Or maybe you're the quiet pensive kind, in which case, put on a floppy hat, find a pole and gaze upon it in a vague, whimsical poet kind of way - that's exactly what I'll be doing this September 21st.

[*1] see disclaimer page; telegraph vs electric

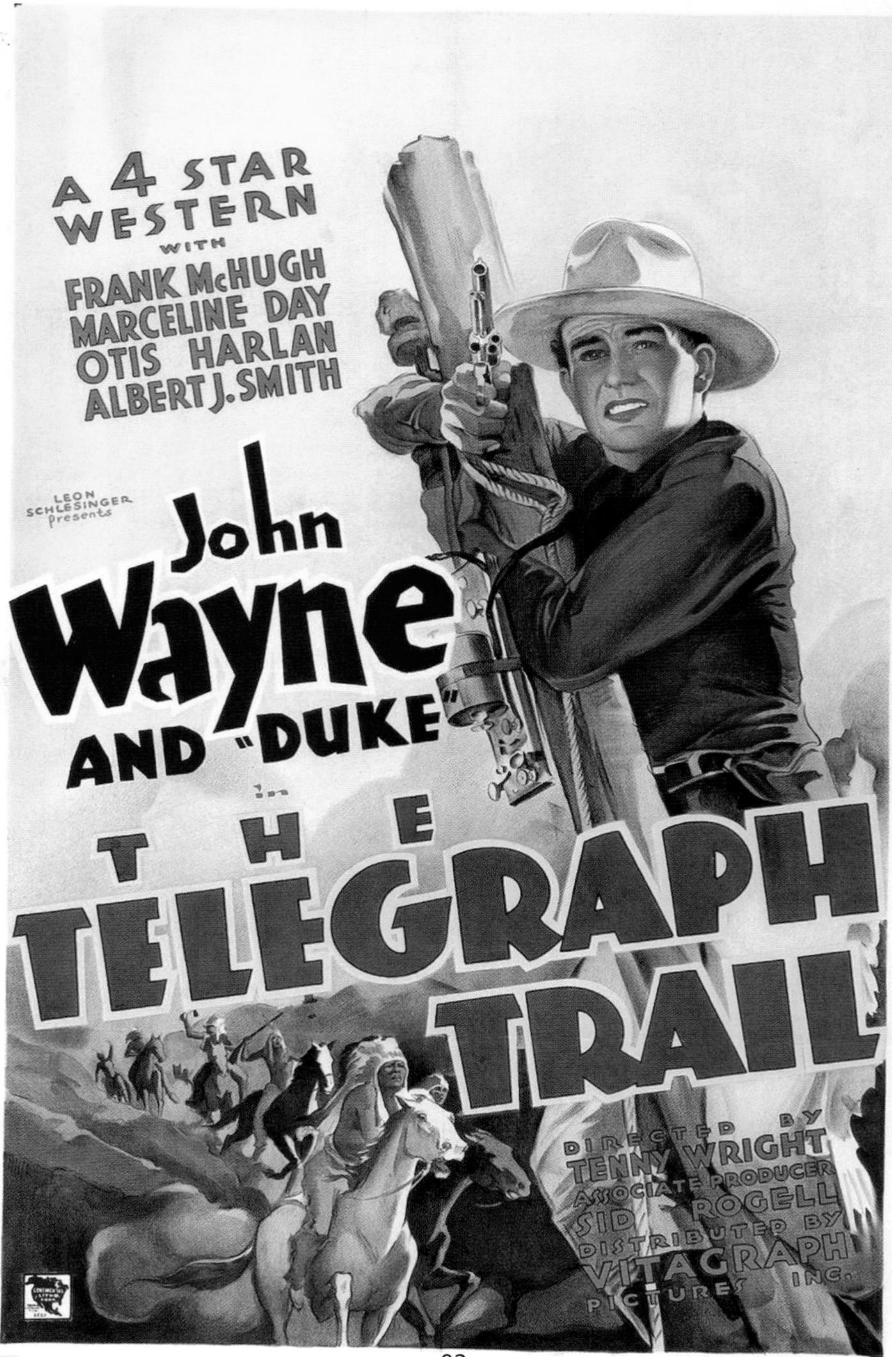

A 4 STAR WESTERN

WITH

FRANK McHUGH
MARCELINE DAY
OTIS HARLAN
ALBERT J. SMITH

LEON SCHLESINGER presents

JOHN Wayne AND "DUKE"

IN

THE TELEGRAPH TRAIL

DIRECTED BY TENNY WRIGHT
ASSOCIATE PRODUCER SID ROGELL
DISTRIBUTED BY VITAGRAPH PICTURES INC.

POLE
of the
WHENEVER
we remember to do one

formerly...

POLE
of the
MONTH

83

P.O.T.W.W.R.T.D.O has always been a very popular part of our society.
It's almost exactly like Match of the Day's Goal of the Month. Except that there are no goals, Gary Lineker has nothing to do with it and ours is not even monthly. But goal does rhyme with pole and that should be enough for anyone.

Should this whole concept need any further explanation, then this book may be a little advanced for you. Here's a few poles from the archive.

December 2015

Malcolm Hindes spotted this and its sister pole alongside a minor road near Harlaw Hill, east of Alnwick in Northumberland. "Perfectly ordinary dropwire is replaced with individual, insulated conductors where it passes under a power line (probably 33kV judging by the insulators). It's the use of individual brackets and a seemingly random mix of plain and "jam-pot" insulators that makes them so striking."

That all sounds like it's in English but from the connoisseur telegraphpoleographer's point of view - it's simply gorgeous.

December 2013

As seen by Kev Currie, aka Lord of the Northern Poles, somewhere between Norfolk and Scotland. Quite possibly on the A68 which nips o'er hill and dale twixt the A1 and Yr Alban (as we say in Wales). Screwtops, double grooves, a finial, er... wires.

February 2011
   This rather seductive looking
pole has been hiding in a field
less than a mile from my house. A
telephoto lens was required to get
this picture.
But anyone who fails to see the
intrinsic feminine beauty of this
power distribution pole in North
Wales - needn't apply to our
society for membership.

   She's called Audrey by the way.
Audrey with the ray-gun eyes.

September 2012

There is a pleasing simplicity yet faintly disturbing asymmetry about this photo of a pole opposite Martyn Fielder's office in Dakar, Senegal. The container depot was built with a distinct lack of foresight. We can assume that they affixed the doors in position from the inside. The pole was there first after all.

And then what sort of backside requires toilet roll the size of that discarded tube?

June 2013

If ever there was a pole photo needs making into a poster it's this one. Karen Frost - who works for (arguably*) the best used telegraph pole supplier in the world - recognised our appreciation of pole aesthetics when she snapped this pic which she titled "Crossed Wires". We're not entirely sure where this is, nor frankly do we care. Ooh Cotgrave in Nottingham to pluck some place out of the air. So presumably this perfectly pleasing parallel perspective pole is around there somewhere.

*Kilgraney Railway Sleepers (they'd argue)

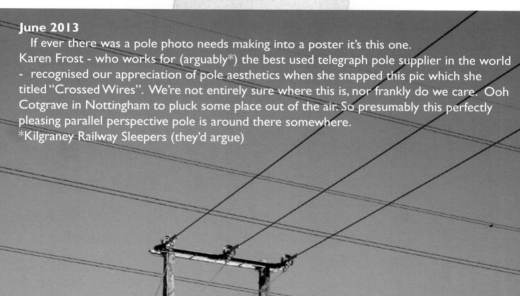

December 2010

You normally only ever see poles like this alongside heritage railway lines. But this is one of a few such poles that follow the B5105 up from Ruthin in Denbighshire. Still sort of in use - the second lower left insulator has a telephone wire attached.

This pole was recently featured in the award*[1] winning documentary film "Telegraph Poles on the B5105".

*[1]

BEST FILM
about
Telegraph Poles
that are on the B5105
2016

87

February 2017

This iconic bridge/pole hybrid can be found where the A519 crosses the Shropshire Union Canal near Norbury, Staffs.

High Bridge No. 39, aka Telegraph Bridge, carries probably one of the most photographed poles in the country – at least by canal boatsfolk.

Canal-dwelling telegraph pole fan Tommy Grimes brought this to our attention.

August 2016

If ever there was a pole worthy of a bus trip to go and see it it's this one. Alex Latham submitted this picture of an olde worlde pole adjacent a cemetery alongside the A167 in Co. Durham. We immediately processed it as a fast track to Pole of the Month. (*Pol des monats/Pôle du mois/ isigxobo lwenyanga*)

Poles as appreciable as this are so rare that it should be a Listed Monument or at least have a Pole Preservation Order put on it. I feel a letter coming on.

Alex, by the way, has the word "exonerd" in her email address. So definitely one of us.

April 2015

This could have qualified as 3 poles of the month. Or pole of three months. April to June say.

Very pleasing to the eye are these fine triplicating power poles at Birstwith, near Harrogate. The subject matter meets almost exactly the definition of the word "triumvirate". This was sent to us by our telegraph pole appreciatiing friend Adrian Trainsett Esq (#0484H).

Triumvirate noun (c)
/traɪ' ^m.vɪ.rət/
A group of three [poles] holding power.

THE TELEGRAPH POLE APPRECIATION SOCIETY

And then there's this one...

This pole and I go back a short lifetime. I long admired its toothy profile grinning out across the field next my house in North Wales. It is shaped thus so as to project the wires it once carried out and over an obstacle such as a hedge. Most often when the pole couldn't be positioned in alignment with others in the run.

Anyway, one day I looked out and it was gone. Presumably forever. The Openreach fairies had visited overnight*[1] and a creosoted bland 8 metre light (L) pole had taken its place.

To the casual reader I would likely come across as inadequate were I to say that really I missed that pole - but oh, how I wailed. Grief is best healed by time or some sort of reunification and some weeks later, whilst cutting back some gorse, I saw through my still tear-blurred eyes my beloved pole. The Openreach fairy had slung it over the hedge and into our field - too lazy to take it back to depot. We were together again. There followed a frenzied period of nursing it back to health: wirebrush, sandpaper, hammerite, bandages for my inevitable DIY wounds.

*[1] Overnight = any time before 11:30am

96

91

...join us, and you can get one of these. Well, don't join us and you can still get one. £8.99*[1]. Comes complete with a handle, pictures on the side and a hole in the middle for your chosen beverage.

Money well spent.

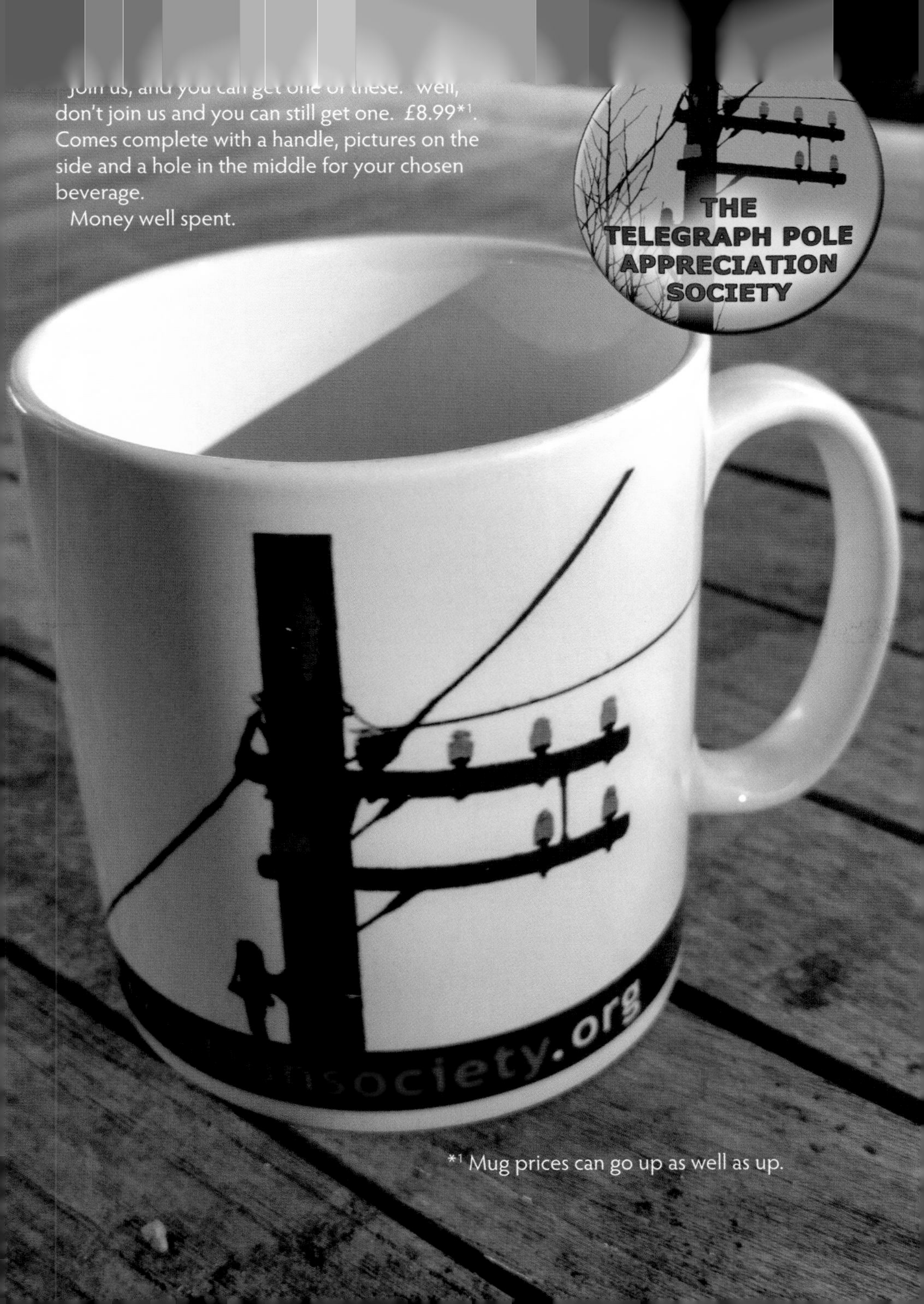

THE
TELEGRAPH POLE
APPRECIATION
SOCIETY

...society.org

*[1] Mug prices can go up as well as up.

Publicity poster for the telephone service, 1935. by Clifford Ellis and Rosemary Ellis. Courtesy of BT Heritage & Archives.

Publicity poster for the telephone service (1943) by artist: N J Sarg. Courtesy of BT Heritage & Archives.

POLEWORD

ACROSS:
2. Distant writing (9)
5. Erect east European(4)
10. Broadsheet daily (9)
11. Subjected to much appreciation (13)
12. see 11 across (13)
13. Sounds like TV barchart (9)
14. Send morse to the easterner (13)
16. Allege Profit for sticky-uppy thing (13)
17. East or left to the shortest river (4)

DOWN
1. Portsmouth and Leicester carry the day (4)
2. agree, help plot the tall thing (13)
3. Great help to solve (9)
4. Grapple hot eel (13)
5. typo legitimisation here (4)
6. Tag helper for news sheet (9)
7. The old 5½ yards (4)
8. Post Office looks east (4)
9. Advance notice in the bush (9)
10. as 3 down.
11. Transmit to first position (13)
15. Fourth link of a chain (4)

TELLY POLES

Y ou would expect television to be a reflection of diversity within the world it represents. This is as true for telegraph poles as it is for people. Outside broadcast shots capture the odd pole in the background or one may feature on the news when it fell on someone's head or a power pole is hit by lightning. But occasionally, and I mean vanishingly rarely, a telegraph pole will feature centre stage.

ENDEAVOUR

Society has shied away from gladiatorial Christians vs Lions blood-letting for prime-time entertainment. We now have to slake our thirst for gore with a myriad murder-solving TV detectives – that and Holby City of course.
Endeavour, a sort of pre-incarnation of telly 'tec Inspector Morse, is one such.

Episode #3 of series 1 entitled "Rocket" produced by Mammoth Screen Productions featured a telegraph pole central to the plot and key to solving the dastardly crime. The story required the props department to reconstruct a GPO pole of the era and to do so they turned to The Telegraph Pole Appreciation Society for expertise[sic].

They hired our entire under-the-bed collection of ceramic insulators and, in

PLOT (Episode #3)
Inspector Jack Regan off the Sweeney must have got promoted or something and left the Flying Squad and ended up becoming Chief Inspector Morse as a telly detective. Things, for me, then got really confusing as he seemed then to become a lot younger and called himself Endeavour. All over my head frankly. But one day, this younger, different looking Jack Regan had to detect a murder in a factory somewhere. Someone got killed. They were involved in killing somebody a few years before. Then someone does something with someone's wife and oh! Endeavour gets his man.

belt-and-braces fashion, also borrowed a shed load from Scottish collector Jack Nesbit. We also furnished them with a myriad close-up photos upon which to base their reconstruction.

Anyway, me and Mrs TPAS borrowed a telly for the event, sat down with a box of past-their-sell-by Maltesers and got ourselves enthralled in the murky world of murder on the box. To be honest I said it was that shifty looking so-and-so all along. I calmly and repeatedly reminded those good people at Mammoth Productions that I wanted my insulators back and lo, a box of Jack Nesbit's smashed insulators arrived in time to hear that he'd received a box of mine in similar condition. Oh how we laughed. Jack was sanguine, me less so.

THE BLACK SHEEP OF WHITEHALL

I have been conducting something of a social experiment these recent years. Namely, to take a myth, perpetuate it, and and hopefully see it on Wikipedia as fact. After all, I managed to get my name listed as Notable Alumni on my old secondary modern school's page.

The adventure began upon receipt of two letters to our august society.

"I'm sure I read somewhere many many years ago that the cross bars on a telegraph pole are always on the side facing London. Any truth in this? I think I read this in a book which had something to do with hiking in the country, saying keep this in mind should you ever get lost. Though I can't see it being correct myself."
Peter C. Nutt

Then shortly afterwards:

"My father was a lorry driver when I was a lad and would tell me that when finding his way coming onto a main road the crossbars on a pole were always put on the side facing London. Is this true? "
Mike Hughes

Well, I'm a great believer in the old adage that there's no smoke without fire. And two people coming up with this notion means that it absolutely must be true. So to ensure the correct propagation of this interesting myth I have ever since always replied in the affirmative. Not only is it true, but the crossbars are actually aimed, using a sextant or something like that to face towards GPO Post Office Tower, 60 Cleveland Mews, London W1 T6.

Further proof, were it needed was the 1942 Ealing comedy, The Black Sheep of Whitehall starring John Mills and Will Hay. During some spurious green screen car chase Mills' character Bobby Jessop notices the cross arms are on the London side. So there.

BRITISH PATHÉ NEWS

A rich source of vitamins C & D as well as an almost infinite number of gratuitous telegraph poles pictures is the British Pathé Library (britishpathe.com). British Pathé was an early newsreel producer leaving a legacy of some 85,000 film clips in thousands of hours of documentary video and some12 million still images. Their entire library is free to watch and procrastinate over. I spent so much time researching on there that the words "Are you writing this flaming book or what?" rattled around my ears for the full two days while I actually wasn't writing this book.

The archive is now run as a commercial enterprise but is at least preserved until the end of time - or the day the sun turns into a red giant and consumes us all in a blazing plasma of death.*[1]

*[1] Whichever comes first.

Below, a scene from **GPO Training (1968)**. There are scores more telegraph pole extracts from the Pathé archive we could share with you, but for reasons of copyright - well, budget actually - we could only run to this one. So in the interests of value-for-money - I've filled the page with it. You may also lilke to check out :

- One Minute News (1946)
- Telegraph Pole Planter (1965)
- Scenes from a Speeding train (1947)
- Any number of the vintage railway films.

The B5105 is a a classic B road meandering through a small bit of North Wales. Its thirteen miles of B-rated tarmac gets people from Ruthin all the way up to Cerrigydrudion. Not only that, but back again if they want to, and even to any one of several places in between. It is popular with cyclists and people who like to dump plastic energy drink bottles - at the last official census 269 Lucozade bottles were counted along its 13 miles of verge. (see b5105.com)
It is a surprisingly safe place to be a cat but less so for motorcyclists who weave its length in droves to test their theories on the after-life.

An award-winning short documentary produced by The Telegraph Pole Appreciation Society examines an ageing run of telegraph poles along this lonely road. "Telegraph Poles on the B5105" is a final look at some old multi-armed poles before they are replaced by modern, ubiquitous and rather bland, armless telephone poles. This film is also available for free via a well known internet video channel - you know, the one that rhymes with chew-boob.

BEST FILM
about
Telegraph Poles
that are on the B5105
2016

THE POLE LINER

The myth that the arms of telegraph poles are always aligned to face London was finally put to bed with Telegraph Pole Films' new sub-feature drama-documentary The Pole Liner. Dramatising an interview with one of the last remaining telegraph pole alignment officers out on his patch somewhere in Wales, this heart-warming film follows a dedicated veteran of the pole runs as he explains something of the nature of his lonely work.

The part of the Alignment Officer was played so powerfully, yet tenderly, by veteran board-treader Stoddart E. Schmelmhausen - middle son of Adolf and Mitzi Schmelmhausen, Weimar cabaret artists. But the role nearly went to Kenneth Brannagh and one can't help but wonder what sort of film we might have been watching had Branagh not completely ignored all contact. With a stellar cast of one, and fine cinematography from someone, and sublime editing throughout, this is surely one to watch out for at some awards somewhere probably.

"When I got the call to play Pole Liner, I didn't have to think about it for one minute" said Schmelmhausen - "it was the role I had been waiting my life for. For the next six months I remained completely in character to get under the skin of that old-timer pole liner. This part drew me down to my deepest draught of method-acting - in fact I still can't shake off that sonofabitch accent. Having seen how the film turned out, I like to think the producers will realise that, ultimately, they made the right choice.

"That Telegraph Pole Films decided to make the film available for free is a superb act of human kindness and thoughtless beauty. Instead of paying through the nose at the multiplex to sit next to someone updating their facebook profile throughout the show, the film-connoisseur can now see it at home whilst updating their own facebook status without being told to turn the blasted thing off."

Stoddart E. Schmelmhausen on the set of "One Flew Over Pikachu's Vest"

The film can be found, in full, via youtube or Vimeo and searching the title The Pole Liner.

THE POLE LINER

"SUPERCALIBRATIOUS"

★★★★★

Mid Wales Express and Star

TELEGRAPH POLE FILMS IN ASSOCIATION WITH THE TELEGRAPH POLE APPRECIATION SOCIETY
A MARTIN EVANS FILM INTRODUCING STODDART E. SCHMELMHAUSEN AS "THE POLE LINER"
CINEMATOGRAPHY KERI EVANS EDIT DOREEN BRACEGIRDLE (Mrs) STUNT COORDINATOR MORRIS SPOON
BASED ON A REAL LIFE MADE-UP STORY BY HERBERT PHLEGM IN CINEMAS 31ST JULY 2016

Sods, odds &

Thanks for this to Andrew Rowsell from BT Openreach - those lovely people who connect up people's lovely telegraph poles so they can have the lovely internet and that. And if I may have said anything hasty about BT and Openreach in the past you have to understand it was in the heat of the moment and I didn't mean it.

All I know about this wire-free telegraph pole is that it is somewhere in the Solent area. Look, there's blue sky so it can't be Wales.

This is either :

1. An interesting new take on finials.
2. A really massive novelty pencil sharpener.
3. A warning to other teddys.

Beer and telegraph poles - what's not to like?

This bespoke pump handle was created by a beer obsessed husband and wife team called Cabin Fever Craft from Michigan.

Despite the bland mass-produced fizzy wee-wee bilge that gets passed off as beer in the UK, America does in fact produce some fantastic ales - real artisan stuff - so hoppy you could ride a bike on it. It's only right that they should have pump handles to boot.

Metal poles...

Well, it's tall, sticky-uppy and got wires all coming out the top. But it isn't made of wood. So meh! really. Might as well be a mini-pylon.

N.F.A. (Not For Appreciation)

Friend, member and regular correspondent is Carter Wall (#0487H) – a Massachutetian*[1] Managing Director of a Boston energy company. So what she doesn't know about poles with wires on could be written on the back of a postage stamp. Not only does Carter's executive boardroom status lend some high-ranking legitimacy to our membership, but she also has friends who are professors. Now, to the rest of us, a professor is someone who didn't stare out of the window during school lessons, did all their homework and who put their hand up because they knew the answer and not because they needed the toilet.

And it was Carter's professorial friend Kate Lingley from the University of Hawaii who took this photo for us. She was on a business trip (see, that's what you also get for paying attention at school) and like me, was amazed at this tangle of electricity.

This aerial spaghetti can be found at the corner of Dongzongbu Hutong and Gongyuan Xiadjie in the Dongcheng district, Beijing.

To me though, seeing a pole under duress like this puts me in mind of those concave-spined donkeys you see in places like Machu Picchu carrying enormously lard-arsed *[2] back-packers and all their glamping gear. So, sadly for the pole, N.F.A.

*[1] made up word.
*[2] and that's swearing

These massive structures support the weight of all the electricity generated by Cefn Croes Windfarm as it crosses the lower slopes of Pumlumon (Eng: Plynlimon) in mid Wales.

On this particular day they had absolutely nothing to do as there wasn't a single breath of wind. So, in an attempt to alleviate their intense boredom, these bipolar poles, near Eisteddfa Gurig farm, took to fishing for clouds. And I was amazed to see this one snag a lovely little cumulus humilis as we passed underneath. It hung onto it for a short while, only to let it go back into the wild once more whereafter the cloud shortly evaporated.

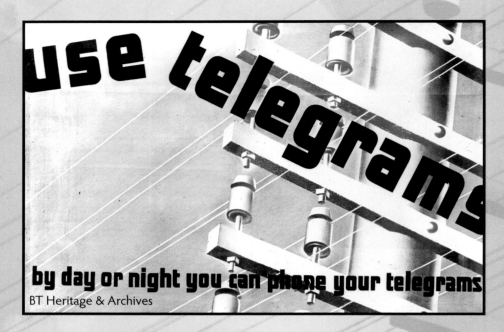

use telegrams

by day or night you can phone your telegrams

BT Heritage & Archives

POST OFFICE *Lines of Communication*

BT Heritage & Archives

April 1950

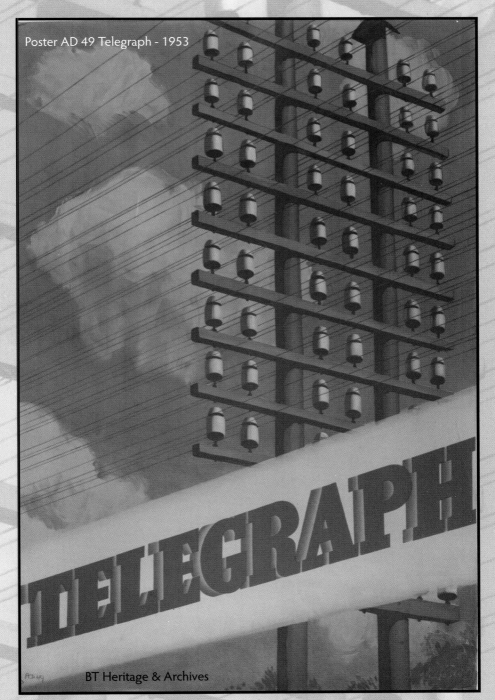

Poster AD 49 Telegraph - 1953

BT Heritage & Archives

W e've previously discussed - or rather I have - that telegraph poles can last a good 100 years with a decent drenching of colourfully carcinogenic creosote. And now that we know how to read the date on a pole let's play telegraph pole...

Time Travel

Britain's newest pole at the time - I watched, mouth agape, as they put this one up in 2016.

2010. In October of this year, the Daily Express runs its 1,000th cure for arthritis headline.

9m light from1986 - the year "Methods in Protein Sequence Analysis" came out. Joyous times.

1972 - into the GPO age. Burtons Wagon Wheels were still over 2ft wide and cost a week's wages.

1966, Bobby Charlton & Nobby Stiles etc. - officially designated the year of the receding hairline.

Woooh! 1953. An adult return to Whitchurch cost 1/2½d. Bloody rip-off Cambrian railway.

We'll skip the 1940s - way too dangerous. 1937 was cut short by strike action to just 11 months.

Ooh! 1936 Wrexham finished mid table in 3rd Division North - pretty much where they are now.

1910. Only another 5 minutes until the Archers finishes on Radio 4 and you can put volume back up.

Well here we are in 1908 already. Henry Ford's Model S motor car wasn't the success he'd hoped for, so he tried again this time adding more wheels and the Model T was born.

In March of this same year, explorer Giles Scott-Heron claims to have reached North Shields - a claim never substantiated.

This 1908 pole still stands in Spalding, Lincs.

This 1904 pole, also from Spalding, was spotted by pole-watcher Gene Kingsley - it looks well enough for its age despite having a 'D' badge as you can see on the photo, right. Note the 14 notches were once crossarms, now it's just a single arm-free pole. 1904 was the year of the Battle of Port Talbot - when a disputed last orders call at the Treorchy Arms resulted in 31 deaths.

1894 Officially the oldest pole according to BT Openreach. The pole was removed and donated to Kirkwall museum not because it was decayed but because the etched lettering could no longer be read by engineers. How lame ! And even sadder is that Kirkwall museum are not really sure what to do with it and so it is in storage in the reserve collection - a lock-up - where's the dignity?

photo credits: Gene Kingsley, Gene Kingsley, BBC

So here it is, lying in state in a Kirkwall shed - that most regal of telegraph poles. Born in 1894 and finally recovered from the rear garden of a house on Franklin Road, Stromness in 2012.

- It has outlived 5 monarchs and is well into No. 6.
- Queen Victoria was on the throne when it was planted. Well, she might have been in her bedroom at the <u>exact</u> time. Or on the loo. In which case, she *was* on the throne. ba-doom tish !
- The Boer War was still only a twinkle in Lord Kitchener's eye at the time.
- Only another 30 Prime Ministers to get to the complete mess we're in today.
- Queues start to form outside Hamley's toy shop, Regent St, London to purchase Tracey Island Activity Playsets which will not come into stock until 1992 - 98 years later.
- Wrexham Association Football Club finish mid table in the third division.

photo courtesy of Orkney Museum

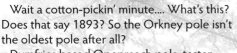

Wait a cotton-pickin' minute.... What's this? Does that say 1893? So the Orkney pole isn't the oldest pole after all?

Dumfries based Openreach pole-tester Stuart Oliver came across this pole with both it and its strut bearing the date 1893. There's an 1899 and an 1896 in the same run.

They're in the Marrburn Exchange area of south wests Scotland on the Penpont to Sanquhar road. Grid Reference : NS8403704610 roughly.

But if that red label is what I think it is then time is of the essence!

DO NOT CLIMB
OR ATTACH ANY
BT PLANT
POLE DUE FOR RECOVERY

photo Stuart Oliver

Retirement

So where do telegraph poles go when they finally hang up their wires? Amazing but so many do actually avoid the pulping yard and enter a productive retirement that doesn't involve working in B&Q.

Fence posts. Perfect, they're already creosoted, though this may be getting a bit thin by this time, and they're the right diameter already. Here's a few I found. The 4th one - an ex 1955 GPO 24ft light is actually the entrance to my own fair garden. With infant holly tree sprouting from the past-its-sell-by top.

What better way to advertise your telegraph component needs than with a retired telegraph pole, complete with eclectic mix of insulator types and a stuffed pigeon atop the tin hat. These sawn-off poles were spotted in front of a house on the A17 and enlivened an otherwise suicide-inducing crawl through bleakest, flattest Lincolnshire; so said our Norwich correspondent, John Cranston.

Chris Jacquier, supposed that we chaps are harmless enough in our pursuit of telegraph poles but worried that this photograph of his back garden fruit patch may completely unhinge some of us. He told us that whilst he failed to gain permission from his domestic authority for a couple of poles to take power to his man-shed - she did capitulate to this vaguely telegraph-polesque structure as a raspberry cane support. Victory of a kind, he said.

Claire Pendrous, from Nottinghamshire is a telegraph pole rescue lady. Exactly like a cat-rescue lady, only with telegraph poles instead. Poles don't get left in a box on her doorstep all that often with a note saying "please look after me". No, Claire is more pro-active than that. She trawls the local undergrowth and pole contractors yards for various parts, then puts them together into meaningful objets d'art for her garden.

This here is one of her finialed highly screw-topped garden creations. Claire was awarded Dame Commander of the Order of the Telegraph Pole in the Telegraph Pole Appreciation Society - New Year's Honours 2015.

A pole that's broken free from its humdrum existence as a holder-aloft of telephone calls could always take to the seaside and grow some mussels. This one has and is a happy pole now in its resting place atop the causeway rocks at Aberystwyth South. It's still there and moves up and down the rocks with each passing winter storm. It is so sodden it probably couldn't float away now if it tried.

Retirement cont'd...

The Telegraph Pole Appreciation Society has a vibrant and enthusiastic Norwich & District branch - whose Honorable Secretary is one Doreen Bracegirdle (Mrs) sister-in-law to Willie Montgomery Stack, erstwhile and almost completely exonerated chair of East Dorset TPAS.

Our Norwich contingent regularly organise coach trips to places of special telegraphic interest. Their recent trip to Southwold found plenty of retired poles....

Hellesdon
Norwich

May 2016

Dear Martin,

I hope you are well.

Did you get those telegraph pole socks we sent you for your birthday? (If you did, then a thank-you card would have been nice. Oh, I'm sorry. You've probably been busy with your 'websight' thingy and I shouldn't nag. I'm sure you get enough of that from you-know-who.)

You asked me to keep you informed of what our local branch has been up to. Well, dear, we had a lovely outing to Southwold last week. The average house there now costs more than half a million pounds. What a pity you didn't listen to me when I told you to think about buying something in the area in the '90s. Imagine what you could buy in Wales now on the proceeds.

I've enclosed Gary Snipe's report of our trip. He took the photographs too. He's allowed to own a camera again, now that he's off the register.

We do hope you'll be able to get over to see us at some stage but, if you can't, rest assured we're taking good care of Pauline. She seems perfectly contented with us here in Hellesdon.

My fondest wishes,

Your loving "Auntie" Doreen.

PS I hope you don't mind, but we actually call her George now. 'Pauline' doesn't seem quite right for an iguana.

TELEGRAPH POLE APPRECIATION SOCIETY
NORWICH AND DISTRICT BRANCH SPRING OUTING, 2016.

Members of the TPAS Norwich and District branch recently visited the delightful Suffolk resort of Southwold.
Like many a coastal town, it has long been a magnet for senior citizens. But now it has become a noted retirement destination … for telegraph poles.
After decades of loyal service these grand old troupers had found their wire-carrying careers at an end. However, rather than spend their remaining years using their free passes to take up all the seats on the buses or holding up queues in the Co-op by counting out £1.93 entirely in coppers or volunteering to work in a charity shop but failing entirely to get to grips with the till, many have taken on useful new jobs. In Southwold they are to be found each day at the harbour, marking out parking spaces, helping shore up the harbour wall, offering a mooring or two and even warning of the presence of underwater cables. That said, a few 'oldies' are still on active BT duty in Southwold (we saw a nice example up an alleyway near a church) and nearby Walberswick (where a 91-year-old pole outside the chapel proudly bears the original DP label). But it's nice to know that, when their time comes, they can look forward to a retirement which doesn't just consist of reading the Daily Mail and tutting.

Gary Snipe, N&D district branch treasurer.

A. GAMES

SEND YOUR GOOD WISHES BY

GREETINGS TELEGRAM

Finials

a finial is
one of these
→

background: James Bancroft

The Victorians, it was, who first started to decorate their telegraph poles with finials. Decorative hats - presumably, to pretty up this ugly [sic] industrial architecture which was springing up across their countryside. They seemed to be in vogue up until the 1930s being slowly replaced by tin hats or just a chamfered cut to keep the rain out.

So, rare, but not vanishingly so. For we with our eyes ever poleward always a pleasing sight and do add something to the top of an otherwise dull pole. The power pole at left is one of a decent run of finialed poles near More Church, south Shropshire - fall off the end of the Long Mynd and you can't miss them.

Later GPO finials were made of metal. And amazingly you can pick one up on eBay for a song. The selection below all sold at recent auctions - they ranged in price from 99p for the wooden one to £9.06. Clearly nobody understands the value of these things. I feel some market-cornering coming on.

Members of the TPAS East Dorset (2015) branch - not to be confused with any previous grouping or organisation bearing the same name - paid a visit to the West Somerset Railway on June 4th, cameras at the ready.

One member was flashing away furiously for the entire 75 minute journey on the old Great Western branch from Bishop's Lydeard to Minehead. The rest of them were just happy to take photographs. But look what they saw when the prints came back from Boots the next morning - the most unusual octagonal beret-esque finials with the poles themselves apparently tapered to make them fit.

Lord of the Northern Poles, aka Kev Currie, is an adroit connoisseur, cataloguer and photographer of vintage telegraph poles and his images are among the finest. Recently, he took the A68 quiet road back to Scotland following a foray into darkest Norfolk. This scenically rolling route manages not only to avoid the customs post but to take in the plethora of strange telegraphic flora and fauna that lines said road. He suggests the A68 for our follow-up tome "Incredible pole-spotting routes in the UK vol 2".

Anyway, this most regal of example is one of the poles he found that day - a bejewelled crown of screw-top insulators topped with a fine finial flourish. Enough to make a queen happy. Sort of.

You couldn't call this a finial, but this tin hat with a Telenduron double-groover on the top is simply magnificent and I just wanted an excuse to get it into my book. So there.

photo: James Bancroft

James, by the way, has the UK's foremost collection of telegraph pole photos. He is an insulator collector, but you can't do one without the other - and on dark winter days I always turn to his pages (myinsulators.com/ukinsulators/) for a pick-me-up. Or the off-licence down the road. One of the two anyway.

Insulators

There are two schools within telegraph pole appreciation:

1. The poles themselves, their look, their shape, the shadows they cast, sillhouettes against a rural skyline, the vanishing point. That kind of thing.
2. The insulators.

It is insulators where the collectors become involved. These delightfully shiny, smooth and variable objects appeal to that certain innate quality of being. Like a bower bird is compelled to line its breeding lek with sparkly blue objects - so the collector lines her bedroom shelf with every My Little Pony™ effigy she can lay her hands on, or Wade Whimsey or Bay City Roller memorabilia.

And so it is with telegraph pole insulators.

It manifests as hobby, but collecting is a well ingrained human trait. I recognise it within myself for sure. It has been made very clear to me that if I bring any more broken telegraph pole bits into our house then my dear wife cannot be held responsible for the acts of non-trivial surgery she will perform on me.

There are two further divisions within insulators themselves: those concerned with insulation of electric power and its transmission; and those concerned with telegraphics.

The division goes even further to insulation material. Whilst most - in the UK - are of a glazed ceramic, there are also bakelite varieties and a bitumen based-material called telenduron. Then there are the manufacturers: Bullers, Denby, Doulton, Taylor Tunnicliff, Wade to name a few. Basically, if the company made porcelain, then they likely made insulators for poles.

This section, though, isn't about the history of insulators - goodness, I could barely sit still/stay awake during history lessons in school, so it'd be hypocritical of me to start preaching history here. No, my concern is, again, with aesthetics and the place of insulators within greater appreciation.

photos James Bancroft

118

Commonly called "double-grooves" of the genus "Cordeaux".
These "Terminators" were the workhorse of the telephone line.

Most common colouring is this white ceramic but also in red, black or brown (see inset)

Variously stamped with GPO or one of many railway companys such as LNER on the top. They are cast with an interior screw thread for fixing to the metal pin.

Variable manufacturers: Bullers, Taylor Tunnicliff etc.

The mainstay of the UK collectors' shelf.

An earthenware insulator, yesterday.

Cordeaux: Named after Mr Cordeaux and his patent improved method of fixing insulators to their bolts. This, to facilitate easier removal for inspection, repair and theft by insulator collectors a century or so later. His method involved screw threaded porcelain interior and a rubber washer. They already had threaded interiors so just for adding the washer bit he got a whole sub-species of ceramic insulator named after him.

These are called "pot-heads" or "screw-tops". They are porcelain and have a screw cap revealing interior connection points often fitted with a fuseholder. These were widely used by both the GPO and also railway company signalling. They make great house-pets. They are loyal, friendly and, most of all, quiet. Also they subsist on little nourishment and consequently you don't need to carry a little poo bag should you take them out for a walk. Photo: James Bancroft.

These are the ebony to picture #1's ivory. They are almost as ubiquitous as their counterparts. They are formed from bitumenous resin which is known to weather badly and they are often brittle. These insulators know everything about you. That they choose to do nothing about it is in your favour.

Photo: James Bancroft.

A hen's tooth. You score 8 points for spotting one of these in the wild. Russ Firth did and so his points are in a jiffy bag and on the way to him as we speak. Made by Wade - the Whimsies people - and mostly only used in east Anglia apparently. One of these delightful purple cordeaux was once the star prize on Anglia TV's quiz show "Sale of the Century".

Photo: Russ Firth.

We received a letter from a lady in Essex who told us she'd inherited two of these green insulators you see here – how lucky is that, all I ever inherited was the lousy Monet that hangs in our bathroom. Anyway, she claimed to know nowt about insulators but quickly worked out from our correspondence that she had something special. Maybe it was my offering to take a taxi for the 200 mile trip just to look at and hold that elusive emerald ceramic which made her nervous.

Anyway, a long story short... some serious email bidding, squabbling and eventual success led to me being the proud owner of this stunning example of a green Denby standard insulator AND a shiny new bank loan. Collector Jack Nesbitt paid handsomely for the other. I wonder does he look at his with the same weird expression on his face as I do?

Marked Fuller & Son, Bow this was found along an SE&CR (S. East & Chatham) railway line. This was of a type unknown before. They were found right on top of the poles and date from around 1880.

A GER pattern insulator marked J Slater Lewis Birkenhead Eng'. This, was found on a Disused railway in Essex, the pole was still standing and this insulator had just fallen off when the pin rusted away.

It was a fondness for old railway artefacts that led South Lincolnshire-based collector and expert Gene Kingsley to his most rare prides and joy (above). And their acquisition gives a clue as to how collectors come upon their booty. Like Gene did for the GER one you could always stand underneath an old pole holding a net and wait 60 years for the pin to rust through and the ceramic to drop. Or... You could be proactive, don a set of linesman's leg irons and climb up to pick them off like so much fruit .

As you travel along a road almost anywhere in the world you may notice vacant pins where once there would have been insulators. They won't have just fallen off or been retired by the telephone company though. They will be basking smug and contented upon a display shelf in someone's living room - glowing warm from their nefarious procuration.

Below the, ahem, acquired collection belonging to James Bancroft and (right) an anonymous collector relieving a pole of it's porcelain fruit. Note the use of leg irons.

photo: James Bancroft oops!

Collecting U.S.A.

Though we are divided by a common language, we are also divided by our dissimilar telegraph ceramics. In the UK the overriding majority of our insulators are porcelain, with a few bitumenesque to makeup the numbers. In the United States they are almost entirely made of glass, coloured, and in a myriad of shapes and forms. And, dare I say it, fantastically collectable. Which is why insulator collecting is so enormous over there. So much so, that as I write these words, the largest collection of insulators and their dealers and enthusiasts have gathered in Colorado Springs for the 48th National Insulator Association Convention, Show & Sales Extravaganza. This is a show on the scale of something you might find at Earls Court or the N.E.C. Birmingham.

Collectable ceramics such as the Wade Whimsies were - cynically one might argue - manufactured to be just that - collectable. With insulators the variance in pattern is due entirely to the environment into which they evolved. They are almost as sea-shells in their variety of form. And as you can see from the small selection below, they are stunning and incredibly shelf-worthy.

Particularly Pleasing Poles

Can't quite put my finger on it, but these poles don't fall into any particular category of telegraphic beauty. They just please me. It's my book, I like them and that's that.

Three electricity distribution poles near Hawes in N. Yorkshire seem to have gathered to exchange information.

Poorly formed musical notes perhaps.

Looks like a bunch of crotchets and semi-quavers can't quite make up their mind what piece of music they want to be.

Jazz looks like it'd take the least to sort out. Yes, something by Miles Davis.

Here's a needy pole if ever there was. This can - or probably past tense by now - could be found just off the lane to Borgie Hotel, which is itself just off the A836 a few miles west of Tongue, Sutherland. Here's the easy way to find it. Go to no-where, start at the outer edges and work your way towards the middle. There you'll find this pole. Does very little nowadays, just a couple of phone lines branching off but just think how splendid this would have looked in its heyday.

As I said, this is my book and I'll put in what I like. This eccentric eclectic electric pole caught my eye at a village called Tillicoutry. A place so unheard of that even the locals just call it "look, it's on the A91 near Stirling".

Come to Stirlingshire - land of the eternally white skies.

Anyway, it's a sort of hybrid of pole types. And I bet if they notice it at all, the Tillicoutrians find it not to their taste. Well it is to mine.

Probably should be in the section called Alignment. There's nothing like a run of power poles for being perfectly in line.

Engineers work to the rule of thumb that for every degree of arc bend in a high-voltage electric cable, there is a one volt drop in potential. So, 90 degree bend = 90v lost.

I'm testing this "fact" out to see if it makes it onto the internet.

This also near Stirling by the way.

Then there's this King George letterbox clinging to a 28ft 1957 GPO pole like a baby monkey to its mum.

This is on the lane to the astronomically named Skyborry near Knighton in Powys, mid Wales. Where God actually does live.

This picture doesn't fit into alignment section on account of the S-bend in the track. And being square it doesn't readily fit into the rectangular pages of this book either. So the layout you see is the best that we could come up with to avoid compromising this fantastically atmospheric photo.

Jon Lewis from Berlin, Connecticut was waiting for a train. None came, so he took this photo of where he was hoping one would come.

The closeness of the poles due to once heavy cables and the complete lack of insulators due to the coloured glass ones that they use in the US being highly collectable.

I've got one of these myself. Legitimately obtained though - I got a friend to steal it.

Sticking with the railway theme - this was taken by a night-time photographer "Prairie" Gerry Pocha from Saskatoon, Saskatchewan.

The railway line disappearing off into the maelstrom of light adds tension and the poles themselves are far out of true and so incite feelings of abandonment. Further drama comes from the sodium flares off to the right. Although the photo is lit with intense light pollution, Saskatchewan is the place to go for nightime darkness and humungous skies.

It is these landscapes that Gerry's camera captures and often by night or at dusk fall. You'll have to summon a thesaurus for superlatives appropriate for some of his pictures - do look him up.

This pole appears to be popping up to surprise you from behind a hedge. Alas, this pole will do so no more - "...cut down in its prime and replaced by an ugly, brutal, dark and sinister new pole erected in its place". Those were the words of a saddened Peter Burton who regularly cycles this lane near Zelah in Cornwall. "This and its sister poles have looked down on passers-by since before WWII and have all been replaced" he told us.

Well it lives on in a tiny way in this tiny corner of a tiny book. And also Peter managed to rescue a couple of the old insulators. I feel an urge to make an analogy to organ transplanting here but it probably wouldn't be appropriate or funny. So I won't.

BT Heritage
& Archives

Trusting sort, me. Of a mind – some might call it daft – that British Telecom is a proper old fashioned British company, with a dusty, tweed jacketed gentleman manager at its head – he's probably called Pat – who looks kindly down on us telephone subscribers and loses sleep when someone's telephone develops a fault or their broadband runs at less than ideal. Pat cycles to work on an old black thing with a basket on the front carrying his briefcase, doffing his cap at everybody he meets. "Morning Mr Pat", they'd cry out. "Morning Mrs Diptheria", he'd chirp back.

I won't listen to anyone telling me they're a boardroom full of slavering capitalists – flinging homeless people into an industrial turbine in order to generate more income. Rubbish. You're wrong I say.

It is with these sepia-tinted spectacles that I bring you this selection of fine images from BT Heritage & Archives...

Thanks to Pat's exemplary leadership, BT conserve and make accessible their entire heritage as far back as 1846. All records produced before 1984 are considered public records and may be searched online or at their purpose-built repository in Holborn Telephone Exchange, London.

Beware though, once you start searching these archives the DIY jobs start to pile up, and personal hygiene tends to take a back seat such is the anorak-inducing nature of their database.

http://www.bt.com/btdigitalarchives

"H" Pole with Linesman
28th March 1934

BT Heritage & Archives

129

Engineer's overhead cable hut,
Haverfordwest, Carmarthenshire.
2nd August 1944

BT Heritage & Archives

Pole number 478 at Hands Cross, W. Sussex.
From a series of poles and overhead Network
running between London and Brighton.
30th July 1931

BT Heritage & Archives

Described simply "Pole Heads. Bad work."
1947

BT Heritage & Archives

Ring type pole head at Raynes Park
16th November 1937

BT Heritage & Archives

Pole line towards remote aerials,
Wick Radio Station, Caithness, Scotland.
3rd November 1937

BT Heritage & Archives

Pole with overhead lines.
Location unknown
1st August 1946

BT Heritage & Archives

National Telephone Company Cork and Douglas Exchange Pole, Ireland circa 1890 - 1910. I swear that's old Sam Archer with the horse.

BT Heritage & Archives

Ornamental pole, Glasgow
Undated.

BT Heritage & Archives

London - Brighton aerial cable
route - Povey Cross roads pole
No. 414
30th July 1941

BT Heritage & Archives

Health & Safety gone mad!
Lineman/Engineer/Trapeze artist
on Overhead Wires, Penarth,
Glamorgan
1905

BT Heritage & Archives   139

Installation of subscribers
telephone. Engineer on
ring type distribution pole
14th January 1954

BT Heritage & Archives

140

"H" Pole with Lineman.
Presumably the same
linesman from page 1 of
this section.
28th February 1938

BT Heritage & Archives

And finally...
If you can't appreciate the wonderful sight of a pollard of poles dancing beneath the stars with the moon and Venus looking on then you probably have no soul. And likely didn't get this far in the book anyway.

"This is a remnant of a railroad signal code line at Rochelle, Illinois along the BNSF. When I saw the Moon, Venus, and the way the poles silhouetted against the sky, I popped on the telephoto and walked down a distance to make all of the elements come together."

Pat Scott, pole and insulator appreciating photographer from St Louis, Missouri.

1. If you came upon this page first and the words are all backwards and weird looking then you are probably holding the book upside down. Please turn the book over and try again.

2. If you came here because you made it all the way through. Then you are most likely "one of us". Go immediately to :

www.telegraphpoleappreciationsociety.org

click the link marked "join us" and await the warm glow*[1] that should soon descend upon you. For a warmer glow*[1] trying buying a mug too.

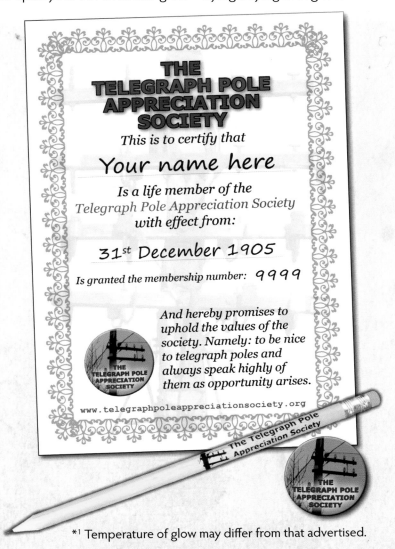

THE TELEGRAPH POLE APPRECIATION SOCIETY

This is to certify that

Your name here

Is a life member of the
Telegraph Pole Appreciation Society
with effect from:

31st December 1905

Is granted the membership number: 9999

And hereby promises to uphold the values of the society. Namely: to be nice to telegraph poles and always speak highly of them as opportunity arises.

www.telegraphpoleappreciationsociety.org

*[1] Temperature of glow may differ from that advertised.

God's Poor Orphans

We are only God's Poor Orphans
But we do our level best.
to keep you all connected and in touch.

In the winter wires are frozen
and we seldom get much rest,
But we don't complain; well, not very much.

We know we're in the service of our monarch
King or Queen.
It's an honour, not a job, so do you see.
That her majesty's the boss, the best boss ever been.

On that all God's Poor Orphans will agree.
We will keep the wires singing,
'Cos you know "It's good to talk"

Keep the tidings winging.
'Quicker to 'phone than to walk'
Greetings merry, news that's sad,
We'll convey them good or bad.

And know at last we did our job
We did it for honour not for a few bob.
We'll end our service with a contented sigh.
And depart for that great Telephone Exchange in the sky.

*by Society Honorary Technical Adviser, Keith S*****